Learning OpenCV 3 Computer Vision with Python

Second Edition

Unleash the power of computer vision with Python using OpenCV

Joe Minichino

Joseph Howse

BIRMINGHAM - MUMBAI

Learning OpenCV 3 Computer Vision with Python
Second Edition

First published: September 2015

Production reference: 1240915

Published by Packt Publishing Ltd.
Livery Place
35 Livery Street
Birmingham B3 2PB, UK.

ISBN 978-1-78528-384-0

www.packtpub.com

Credits

Authors
Joe Minichino
Joseph Howse

Reviewers
Nandan Banerjee
Tian Cao
Brandon Castellano
Haojian Jin
Adrian Rosebrock

Commissioning Editor
Akram Hussain

Acquisition Editors
Vivek Anantharaman
Prachi Bisht

Content Development Editor
Ritika Singh

Technical Editors
Novina Kewalramani
Shivani Kiran Mistry

Copy Editor
Sonia Cheema

Project Coordinator
Milton Dsouza

Proofreader
Safis Editing

Indexer
Monica Ajmera Mehta

Graphics
Disha Haria

Production Coordinator
Arvindkumar Gupta

Cover Work
Arvindkumar Gupta

About the Authors

Joe Minichino is a computer vision engineer for Hoolux Medical by day and a developer of the NoSQL database LokiJS by night. On weekends, he is a heavy metal singer/songwriter. He is a passionate programmer who is immensely curious about programming languages and technologies and constantly experiments with them. At Hoolux, Joe leads the development of an Android computer vision-based advertising platform for the medical industry.

Born and raised in Varese, Lombardy, Italy, and coming from a humanistic background in philosophy (at Milan's Università Statale), Joe has spent his last 11 years living in Cork, Ireland, which is where he became a computer science graduate at the Cork Institute of Technology.

I am immensely grateful to my partner, Rowena, for always encouraging me, and also my two little daughters for inspiring me. A big thank you to the collaborators and editors of this book, especially Joe Howse, Adrian Roesbrock, Brandon Castellano, the OpenCV community, and the people at Packt Publishing.

Joseph Howse lives in Canada. During the winters, he grows his beard, while his four cats grow their thick coats of fur. He loves combing his cats every day and sometimes, his cats also pull his beard.

He has been writing for Packt Publishing since 2012. His books include *OpenCV for Secret Agents*, *OpenCV Blueprints*, *Android Application Programming with OpenCV 3*, *OpenCV Computer Vision with Python*, and *Python Game Programming by Example*.

When he is not writing books or grooming his cats, he provides consulting, training, and software development services through his company, Nummist Media (http://nummist.com).

About the Reviewers

Nandan Banerjee has a bachelor's degree in computer science and a master's in robotics engineering. He started working with Samsung Electronics right after graduation. He worked for a year at its R&D centre in Bangalore. He also worked in the WPI-CMU team on the Boston Dynamics' robot, Atlas, for the DARPA Robotics Challenge. He is currently working as a robotics software engineer in the technology organization at iRobot Corporation. He is an embedded systems and robotics enthusiast with an inclination toward computer vision and motion planning. He has experience in various languages, including C, C++, Python, Java, and Delphi. He also has a substantial experience in working with ROS, OpenRAVE, OpenCV, PCL, OpenGL, CUDA and the Android SDK.

> I would like to thank the author and publisher for coming out with this wonderful book.

Tian Cao is pursuing his PhD in computer science at the University of North Carolina in Chapel Hill, USA, and working on projects related to image analysis, computer vision, and machine learning.

> I dedicate this work to my parents and girlfriend.

Brandon Castellano is a student from Canada pursuing an MESc in electrical engineering at the University of Western Ontario, City of London, Canada. He received his BESc in the same subject in 2012. The focus of his research is in parallel processing and GPGPU/FPGA optimization for real-time implementations of image processing algorithms. Brandon also works for Eagle Vision Systems Inc., focusing on the use of real-time image processing for robotics applications.

While he has been using OpenCV and C++ for more than 5 years, he has also been advocating the use of Python frequently in his research, most notably, for its rapid speed of development, allowing low-level interfacing with complex systems. This is evident in his open source projects hosted on GitHub, for example, PySceneDetect, which is mostly written in Python. In addition to image/video processing, he has also worked on implementations of three-dimensional displays as well as the software tools to support the development of such displays.

In addition to posting technical articles and tutorials on his website (`http://www.bcastell.com`), he participates in a variety of both open and closed source projects and contributes to GitHub under the username Breakthrough (`http://www.github.com/Breakthrough`). He is an active member of the Super User and Stack Overflow communities (under the name Breakthrough), and can be contacted directly via his website.

I would like to thank all my friends and family for their patience during the past few years (especially my parents, Peter and Lori, and my brother, Mitchell). I could not have accomplished everything without their continued love and support. I can't ever thank everyone enough.

I would also like to extend a special thanks to all of the developers that contribute to open source software libraries, specifically OpenCV, which help bring the development of cutting-edge software technology closer to all the software developers around the world, free of cost. I would also like to thank those people who help write documentation, submit bug reports, and write tutorials/books (especially the author of this book!). Their contributions are vital to the success of any open source project, especially one that is as extensive and complex as OpenCV.

Haojian Jin is a software engineer/researcher at Yahoo! Labs, Sunnyvale, CA. He looks primarily at building new systems of what's possible on commodity mobile devices (or with minimum hardware changes). To create things that don't exist today, he spends large chunks of his time playing with signal processing, computer vision, machine learning, and natural language processing and using them in interesting ways. You can find more about him at http://shift-3.com/

Adrian Rosebrock is an author and blogger at http://www.pyimagesearch.com/. He holds a PhD in computer science from the University of Maryland, Baltimore County, USA, with a focus on computer vision and machine learning.

He has consulted for the National Cancer Institute to develop methods that automatically predict breast cancer risk factors using breast histology images. He has also authored a book, *Practical Python and OpenCV* (http://pyimg.co/x7ed5), on the utilization of Python and OpenCV to build real-world computer vision applications.

www.PacktPub.com

Support files, eBooks, discount offers, and more

For support files and downloads related to your book, please visit www.PacktPub.com.

Did you know that Packt offers eBook versions of every book published, with PDF and ePub files available? You can upgrade to the eBook version at www.PacktPub.com and as a print book customer, you are entitled to a discount on the eBook copy. Get in touch with us at service@packtpub.com for more details.

At www.PacktPub.com, you can also read a collection of free technical articles, sign up for a range of free newsletters and receive exclusive discounts and offers on Packt books and eBooks.

https://www2.packtpub.com/books/subscription/packtlib

Do you need instant solutions to your IT questions? PacktLib is Packt's online digital book library. Here, you can search, access, and read Packt's entire library of books.

Why subscribe?

- Fully searchable across every book published by Packt
- Copy and paste, print, and bookmark content
- On demand and accessible via a web browser

Free access for Packt account holders

If you have an account with Packt at www.PacktPub.com, you can use this to access PacktLib today and view 9 entirely free books. Simply use your login credentials for immediate access.

Table of Contents

Preface

OpenCV 3 is a state-of-the-art computer vision library that is used for a variety of image and video processing operations. Some of the more spectacular and futuristic features, such as face recognition or object tracking, are easily achievable with OpenCV 3. Learning the basic concepts behind computer vision algorithms, models, and OpenCV's API will enable the development of all sorts of real-world applications, including security and surveillance tools.

Starting with basic image processing operations, this book will take you through a journey that explores advanced computer vision concepts. Computer vision is a rapidly evolving science whose applications in the real world are exploding, so this book will appeal to computer vision novices as well as experts of the subject who want to learn about the brand new OpenCV 3.0.0.

What this book covers

Chapter 1, *Setting Up OpenCV*, explains how to set up OpenCV 3 with Python on different platforms. It will also troubleshoot common problems.

Chapter 2, *Handling Files, Cameras, and GUIs*, introduces OpenCV's I/O functionalities. It will also discuss the concept of a project and the beginnings of an object-oriented design for this project.

Chapter 3, *Processing Images with OpenCV 3*, presents some techniques required to alter images, such as detecting skin tone in an image, sharpening an image, marking contours of subjects, and detecting crosswalks using a line segment detector.

Chapter 4, *Depth Estimation and Segmentation*, shows you how to use data from a depth camera to identify foreground and background regions, such that we can limit an effect to only the foreground or background.

Chapter 5, *Detecting and Recognizing Faces*, introduces some of OpenCV's face detection functionalities, along with the data files that define particular types of trackable objects.

Chapter 6, *Retrieving Images and Searching Using Image Descriptors*, shows how to detect the features of an image with the help of OpenCV and make use of them to match and search for images.

Chapter 7, *Detecting and Recognizing Objects*, introduces the concept of detecting and recognizing objects, which is one of the most common challenges in computer vision.

Chapter 8, *Tracking Objects*, explores the vast topic of object tracking, which is the process of locating a moving object in a movie or video feed with the help of a camera.

Chapter 9, *Neural Networks with OpenCV – an Introduction*, introduces you to Artificial Neural Networks in OpenCV and illustrates their usage in a real-life application.

What you need for this book

You simply need a relatively recent computer, as the first chapter will guide you through the installation of all the necessary software. A webcam is highly recommended, but not necessary.

Who this book is for

This book is aimed at programmers with working knowledge of Python as well as people who want to explore the topic of computer vision using the OpenCV library. No previous experience of computer vision or OpenCV is required. Programming experience is recommended.

Conventions

In this book, you will find a number of text styles that distinguish between different kinds of information. Here are some examples of these styles and an explanation of their meaning.

Code words in text, database table names, folder names, filenames, file extensions, pathnames, dummy URLs, user input, and Twitter handles are shown as follows: "We can include other contexts through the use of the `include` directive."

A block of code is set as follows:

```
import cv2
import numpy as np

img = cv2.imread('images/chess_board.png')
gray = cv2.cvtColor(img, cv2.COLOR_BGR2GRAY)
gray = np.float32(gray)
dst = cv2.cornerHarris(gray, 2, 23, 0.04)
```

When we wish to draw your attention to a particular part of a code block, the relevant lines or items are set in bold:

```
img = cv2.imread('images/chess_board.png')
gray = cv2.cvtColor(img, cv2.COLOR_BGR2GRAY)
gray = np.float32(gray)
dst = cv2.cornerHarris(gray, 2, 23, 0.04)
```

Any command-line input or output is written as follows:

```
mkdir build && cd build
cmake D CMAKE_BUILD_TYPE=Release -DOPENCV_EXTRA_MODULES_PATH=<opencv_
contrib>/modules  D CMAKE_INSTALL_PREFIX=/usr/local ..
make
```

New terms and **important words** are shown in bold. Words that you see on the screen, for example, in menus or dialog boxes, appear in the text like this: " On Windows Vista / Windows 7 / Windows 8, click on the **Start** menu."

 Warnings or important notes appear in a box like this.

 Tips and tricks appear like this.

Reader feedback

Feedback from our readers is always welcome. Let us know what you think about this book—what you liked or disliked. Reader feedback is important for us as it helps us develop titles that you will really get the most out of.

To send us general feedback, simply e-mail feedback@packtpub.com, and mention the book's title in the subject of your message.

If there is a topic that you have expertise in and you are interested in either writing or contributing to a book, see our author guide at www.packtpub.com/authors.

Customer support

Now that you are the proud owner of a Packt book, we have a number of things to help you to get the most from your purchase.

Downloading the example code

You can download the example code files from your account at http://www.packtpub.com for all the Packt Publishing books you have purchased. If you purchased this book elsewhere, you can visit http://www.packtpub.com/support and register to have the files e-mailed directly to you.

Errata

Although we have taken every care to ensure the accuracy of our content, mistakes do happen. If you find a mistake in one of our books—maybe a mistake in the text or the code—we would be grateful if you could report this to us. By doing so, you can save other readers from frustration and help us improve subsequent versions of this book. If you find any errata, please report them by visiting http://www.packtpub.com/submit-errata, selecting your book, clicking on the **Errata Submission Form** link, and entering the details of your errata. Once your errata are verified, your submission will be accepted and the errata will be uploaded to our website or added to any list of existing errata under the Errata section of that title.

To view the previously submitted errata, go to https://www.packtpub.com/books/content/support and enter the name of the book in the search field. The required information will appear under the **Errata** section.

Piracy

Piracy of copyrighted material on the Internet is an ongoing problem across all media. At Packt, we take the protection of our copyright and licenses very seriously. If you come across any illegal copies of our works in any form on the Internet, please provide us with the location address or website name immediately so that we can pursue a remedy.

Please contact us at copyright@packtpub.com with a link to the suspected pirated material.

We appreciate your help in protecting our authors and our ability to bring you valuable content.

Questions

If you have a problem with any aspect of this book, you can contact us at questions@packtpub.com, and we will do our best to address the problem.

1
Setting Up OpenCV

You picked up this book so you may already have an idea of what OpenCV is. Maybe, you heard of Sci-Fi-sounding features, such as face detection, and got intrigued. If this is the case, you've made the perfect choice. **OpenCV** stands for **Open Source Computer Vision**. It is a free computer vision library that allows you to manipulate images and videos to accomplish a variety of tasks from displaying the feed of a webcam to potentially teaching a robot to recognize real-life objects.

In this book, you will learn to leverage the immense potential of OpenCV with the Python programming language. Python is an elegant language with a relatively shallow learning curve and very powerful features. This chapter is a quick guide to setting up Python 2.7, OpenCV, and other related libraries. After setup, we also look at OpenCV's Python sample scripts and documentation.

If you wish to skip the installation process and jump right into action, you can download the **virtual machine** (**VM**) I've made available at `http://techfort.github.io/pycv/`.

This file is compatible with VirtualBox, a free-to-use virtualization application that lets you build and run VMs. The VM I've built is based on Ubuntu Linux 14.04 and has all the necessary software installed so that you can start coding right away.

This VM requires at least 2 GB of RAM to run smoothly, so make sure that you allocate at least 2 (but, ideally, more than 4) GB of RAM to the VM, which means that your host machine will need at least 6 GB of RAM to sustain it.

The following related libraries are covered in this chapter:

- **NumPy**: This library is a dependency of OpenCV's Python bindings. It provides numeric computing functionality, including efficient arrays.

- **SciPy**: This library is a scientific computing library that is closely related to NumPy. It is not required by OpenCV, but it is useful for manipulating data in OpenCV images.

- **OpenNI**: This library is an optional dependency of OpenCV. It adds the support for certain depth cameras, such as Asus XtionPRO.

- **SensorKinect**: This library is an OpenNI plugin and optional dependency of OpenCV. It adds support for the Microsoft Kinect depth camera.

For this book's purposes, OpenNI and SensorKinect can be considered optional. They are used throughout *Chapter 4*, *Depth Estimation and Segmentation*, but are not used in the other chapters or appendices.

 This book focuses on OpenCV 3, the new major release of the OpenCV library. All additional information about OpenCV is available at `http://opencv.org`, and its documentation is available at `http://docs.opencv.org/master`.

Choosing and using the right setup tools

We are free to choose various setup tools, depending on our operating system and how much configuration we want to do. Let's take an overview of the tools for Windows, Mac, Ubuntu, and other Unix-like systems.

Installation on Windows

Windows does not come with Python preinstalled. However, installation wizards are available for precompiled Python, NumPy, SciPy, and OpenCV. Alternatively, we can build from a source. OpenCV's build system uses CMake for configuration and either Visual Studio or MinGW for compilation.

If we want support for depth cameras, including Kinect, we should first install OpenNI and SensorKinect, which are available as precompiled binaries with installation wizards. Then, we must build OpenCV from a source.

 The precompiled version of OpenCV does not offer support for depth cameras.

On Windows, OpenCV 2 offers better support for 32-bit Python than 64-bit Python; however, with the majority of computers sold today being 64-bit systems, our instructions will refer to 64-bit. All installers have 32-bit versions available from the same site as the 64-bit.

Some of the following steps refer to editing the system's PATH variable. This task can be done in the **Environment Variables** window of **Control Panel**.

1. On Windows Vista / Windows 7 / Windows 8, click on the **Start** menu and launch **Control Panel**. Now, navigate to **System** and **Security | System | Advanced system settings**. Click on the **Environment Variables...** button.

2. On Windows XP, click on the **Start** menu and navigate to **Control Panel | System**. Select the **Advanced** tab. Click on the **Environment Variables...** button.

3. Now, under **System variables**, select **Path** and click on the **Edit...** button.

4. Make changes as directed.

5. To apply the changes, click on all the **OK** buttons (until we are back in the main window of **Control Panel**).

6. Then, log out and log back in (alternatively, reboot).

Using binary installers (no support for depth cameras)

You can choose to install Python and its related libraries separately if you prefer; however, there are Python distributions that come with installers that will set up the entire SciPy stack (which includes Python and NumPy), which make it very trivial to set up the development environment.

One such distribution is Anaconda Python (downloadable at `http://09c8d0b2229f813c1b93c95ac804525aac4b6dba79b00b39d1d3.r79.cf1.rackcdn.com/Anaconda-2.1.0Windows-x86_64.exe`). Once the installer is downloaded, run it and remember to add the path to the Anaconda installation to your PATH variable following the preceding procedure.

Here are the steps to set up Python7, NumPy, SciPy, and OpenCV:

1. Download and install the 32-bit Python 2.7.9 from `https://www.python.org/ftp/python/2.7.9/python-2.7.9.amd64.msi`.

2. Download and install NumPy 1.6.2 from `http://www.lfd.uci.edu/~gohlke/pythonlibs/#numpyhttp://sourceforge.net/projects/numpy/files/NumPy/1.6.2/numpy-1.6.2-win32-superpack-python2.7.exe/download` (note that installing NumPy on Windows 64-bit is a bit tricky due to the lack of a 64-bit Fortran compiler on Windows, which NumPy depends on. The binary at the preceding link is unofficial).

3. Download and install SciPy 11.0 from `http://www.lfd.uci.edu/~gohlke/pythonlibs/#scipyhttp://sourceforge.net/projects/scipy/files/scipy/0.11.0/scipy-0.11.0win32-superpack-python2.7.exe/download` (this is the same as NumPy and these are community installers).

4. Download the self-extracting ZIP of OpenCV 3.0.0 from `https://github.com/Itseez/opencv`. Run this ZIP, and when prompted, enter a destination folder, which we will refer to as `<unzip_destination>`. A subfolder, `<unzip_destination>\opencv`, is created.

5. Copy `<unzip_destination>\opencv\build\python\2.7\cv2.pyd` to `C:\Python2.7\Lib\site-packages` (assuming that we had installed Python 2.7 to the default location). If you installed Python 2.7 with Anaconda, use the Anaconda installation folder instead of the default Python installation. Now, the new Python installation can find OpenCV.

6. A final step is necessary if we want Python scripts to run using the new Python installation by default. Edit the system's PATH variable and append `;C:\Python2.7` (assuming that we had installed Python 2.7 to the default location) or your Anaconda installation folder. Remove any previous Python paths, such as `;C:\Python2.6`. Log out and log back in (alternatively, reboot).

Using CMake and compilers

Windows does not come with any compilers or CMake. We need to install them. If we want support for depth cameras, including Kinect, we also need to install OpenNI and SensorKinect.

Let's assume that we have already installed 32-bit Python 2.7, NumPy, and SciPy either from binaries (as described previously) or from a source. Now, we can proceed with installing compilers and CMake, optionally installing OpenNI and SensorKinect, and then building OpenCV from the source:

1. Download and install CMake 3.1.2 from `http://www.cmake.org/files/v3.1/cmake-3.1.2-win32-x86.exe`. When running the installer, select either **Add CMake to the system PATH for all users** or **Add CMake to the system PATH for current user**. Don't worry about the fact that a 64-bit version of CMake is not available CMake is only a configuration tool and does not perform any compilations itself. Instead, on Windows, it creates project files that can be opened with Visual Studio.

2. Download and install Microsoft Visual Studio 2013 (the Desktop edition if you are working on Windows 7) from `https://www.visualstudio.com/products/free-developer-offers-vs.aspx?slcid=0x409&type=web` or `MinGW`.

    Note that you will need to sign in with your Microsoft account and if you don't have one, you can create one on the spot. Install the software and reboot after installation is complete.

    For MinGW, get the installer from `http://sourceforge.net/projects/mingw/files/Installer/mingw-get-setup.exe/download` and `http://sourceforge.net/projects/mingw/files/OldFiles/mingw-get-inst/mingw-get-inst-20120426/mingw-get-inst-20120426.exe/download`. When running the installer, make sure that the destination path does not contain spaces and that the optional C++ compiler is included. Edit the system's `PATH` variable and append `;C:\MinGW\bin` (assuming that MinGW is installed to the default location). Reboot the system.

3. Optionally, download and install OpenNI 1.5.4.0 from the links provided in the GitHub homepage of OpenNI at `https://github.com/OpenNI/OpenNI`.

4. You can download and install SensorKinect 0.93 from `https://github.com/avin2/SensorKinect/blob/unstable/Bin/SensorKinect093-Bin-Win32-v5.1.2.1.msi?raw=true` (32-bit). Alternatively, for 64-bit Python, download the setup from `https://github.com/avin2/SensorKinect/blob/unstable/Bin/SensorKinect093-Bin-Win64-v5.1.2.1.msi?raw=true` (64-bit). Note that this repository has been inactive for more than three years.

5. Download the self-extracting ZIP of OpenCV 3.0.0 from `https://github.com/Itseez/opencv`. Run the self-extracting ZIP, and when prompted, enter any destination folder, which we will refer to as `<unzip_destination>`. A subfolder, `<unzip_destination>\opencv`, is then created.

6. Open Command Prompt and make another folder where our build will go using this command:

```
> mkdir<build_folder>
```

Change the directory of the `build` folder:

```
> cd <build_folder>
```

7. Now, we are ready to configure our build. To understand all the options, we can read the code in `<unzip_destination>\opencv\CMakeLists.txt`. However, for this book's purposes, we only need to use the options that will give us a release build with Python bindings, and optionally, depth camera support via OpenNI and SensorKinect.

8. Open CMake (`cmake-gui`) and specify the location of the source code of OpenCV and the folder where you would like to build the library. Click on **Configure**. Select the project to be generated. In this case, select Visual Studio 12 (which corresponds to Visual Studio 2013). After CMake has finished configuring the project, it will output a list of build options. If you see a red background, it means that your project may need to be reconfigured: CMake might report that it has failed to find some dependencies. Many of OpenCV's dependencies are optional, so do not be too concerned yet.

> If the build fails to complete or you run into problems later, try installing missing dependencies (often available as prebuilt binaries), and then rebuild OpenCV from this step.
>
> You have the option of selecting/deselecting build options (according to the libraries you have installed on your machine) and click on **Configure** again, until you get a clear background (white).

9. At the end of this process, you can click on **Generate**, which will create an `OpenCV.sln` file in the folder you've chosen for the build. You can then navigate to `<build_folder>/OpenCV.sln` and open the file with Visual Studio 2013, and proceed with building the project, `ALL_BUILD`. You will need to build both the **Debug** and **Release** versions of OpenCV, so go ahead and build the library in the **Debug** mode, then select **Release** and rebuild it (*F7* is the key to launch the build).

10. At this stage, you will have a `bin` folder in the OpenCV build directory, which will contain all the generated `.dll` files that will allow you to include OpenCV in your projects.

Alternatively, for MinGW, run the following command:

```
> cmake -D:CMAKE_BUILD_TYPE=RELEASE -D:WITH_OPENNI=ON -G
"MinGWMakefiles" <unzip_destination>\opencv
```

If OpenNI is not installed, omit `-D:WITH_OPENNI=ON`. (In this case, depth cameras will not be supported.) If OpenNI and SensorKinect are installed to nondefault locations, modify the command to include `-D:OPENNI_ LIB_DIR=<openni_install_destination>\Lib -D:OPENNI_INCLUDE_ DIR=<openni_install_destination>\Include -D:OPENNI_PRIME_ SENSOR_MODULE_BIN_DIR=<sensorkinect_install_destination>\ Sensor\Bin`.

Alternatively, for MinGW, run this command:

```
> mingw32-make
```

11. Copy `<build_folder>\lib\Release\cv2.pyd` (from a Visual Studio build) or `<build_folder>\lib\cv2.pyd` (from a MinGW build) to `<python_ installation_folder>\site-packages`.

12. Finally, edit the system's `PATH` variable and append `;<build_folder>/bin/ Release` (for a Visual Studio build) or `;<build_folder>/bin` (for a MinGW build). Reboot your system.

Installing on OS X

Some versions of Mac used to come with a version of Python 2.7 preinstalled that were customized by Apple for a system's internal needs. However, this has changed and the standard version of OS X ships with a standard installation of Python. On `python.org`, you can also find a universal binary that is compatible with both the new Intel systems and the legacy PowerPC.

> You can obtain this installer at `https://www.python.org/ downloads/release/python-279/` (refer to the Mac OS X 32-bit PPC or the Mac OS X 64-bit Intel links). Installing Python from the downloaded `.dmg` file will simply overwrite your current system installation of Python.

For Mac, there are several possible approaches for obtaining standard Python 2.7, NumPy, SciPy, and OpenCV. All approaches ultimately require OpenCV to be compiled from a source using Xcode Developer Tools. However, depending on the approach, this task is automated for us in various ways by third-party tools. We will look at these kinds of approaches using MacPorts or Homebrew. These tools can potentially do everything that CMake can, plus they help us resolve dependencies and separate our development libraries from system libraries.

I recommend MacPorts, especially if you want to compile OpenCV with depth camera support via OpenNI and SensorKinect. Relevant patches and build scripts, including some that I maintain, are ready-made for MacPorts. By contrast, Homebrew does not currently provide a ready-made solution to compile OpenCV with depth camera support.

Before proceeding, let's make sure that the Xcode Developer Tools are properly set up:

1. Download and install Xcode from the Mac App Store or `https://developer.apple.com/xcode/downloads/`. During installation, if there is an option to install **Command Line Tools**, select it.

2. Open Xcode and accept the license agreement.

3. A final step is necessary if the installer does not give us the option to install **Command Line Tools**. Navigate to **Xcode** | **Preferences** | **Downloads**, and click on the **Install** button next to **Command Line Tools**. Wait for the installation to finish and quit Xcode.

Alternatively, you can install Xcode command-line tools by running the following command (in the terminal):

```
$ xcode-select -install
```

Now, we have the required compilers for any approach.

Using MacPorts with ready-made packages

We can use the MacPorts package manager to help us set up Python 2.7, NumPy, and OpenCV. MacPorts provides terminal commands that automate the process of downloading, compiling, and installing various pieces of **open source software** (**OSS**). MacPorts also installs dependencies as needed. For each piece of software, the dependencies and build recipes are defined in a configuration file called a Portfile. A MacPorts repository is a collection of **Portfiles**.

Starting from a system where Xcode and its command-line tools are already set up, the following steps will give us an OpenCV installation via MacPorts:

1. Download and install MacPorts from `http://www.macports.org/install.php`.

2. If you want support for the Kinect depth camera, you need to tell MacPorts where to download the custom Portfiles that I have written. To do so, edit `/opt/local/etc/macports/sources.conf` (assuming that MacPorts is installed to the default location). Just above the line, `rsync://rsync.macports.org/release/ports/ [default]`, add the following line:

   ```
   http://nummist.com/opencv/ports.tar.gz
   ```

   Save the file. Now, MacPorts knows that it has to search for Portfiles in my online repository first, and then the default online repository.

3. Open the terminal and run the following command to update MacPorts:

   ```
   $ sudo port selfupdate
   ```

   When prompted, enter your password.

4. Now (if we are using my repository), run the following command to install OpenCV with Python 2.7 bindings and support for depth cameras, including Kinect:

   ```
   $ sudo port install opencv +python27 +openni_sensorkinect
   ```

   Alternatively (with or without my repository), run the following command to install OpenCV with Python 2.7 bindings and support for depth cameras, excluding Kinect:

   ```
   $ sudo port install opencv +python27 +openni
   ```

> Dependencies, including Python 2.7, NumPy, OpenNI, and (in the first example) SensorKinect, are automatically installed as well.
>
> By adding `+python27` to the command, we specify that we want the `opencv` variant (build configuration) with Python 2.7 bindings. Similarly, `+openni_sensorkinect` specifies the variant with the broadest possible support for depth cameras via OpenNI and SensorKinect. You may omit `+openni_sensorkinect` if you do not intend to use depth cameras, or you may replace it with `+openni` if you do intend to use OpenNI-compatible depth cameras but just not Kinect. To see the full list of the available variants before installing, we can enter the following command:
>
> ```
> $ port variants opencv
> ```
>
> Depending on our customization needs, we can add other variants to the `install` command. For even more flexibility, we can write our own variants (as described in the next section).

5. Also, run the following command to install SciPy:

    ```
    $ sudo port install py27-scipy
    ```

6. The Python installation's executable is named `python2.7`. If we want to link the default `python` executable to `python2.7`, let's also run this command:

    ```
    $ sudo port install python_select
    ```

    ```
    $ sudo port select python python27
    ```

Using MacPorts with your own custom packages

With a few extra steps, we can change the way that MacPorts compiles OpenCV or any other piece of software. As previously mentioned, MacPorts' build recipes are defined in configuration files called Portfiles. By creating or editing Portfiles, we can access highly configurable build tools, such as CMake, while also benefitting from MacPorts' features, such as dependency resolution.

Let's assume that we already have MacPorts installed. Now, we can configure MacPorts to use the custom Portfiles that we write:

1. Create a folder somewhere to hold our custom Portfiles. We will refer to this folder as `<local_repository>`.

2. Edit the `/opt/local/etc/macports/sources.conf` file (assuming that MacPorts is installed to the default location). Just above the `rsync://rsync.macports.org/release/ports/ [default]` line, add this line:

    ```
    file://<local_repository>
    ```

    For example, if `<local_repository>` is `/Users/Joe/Portfiles`, add the following line:

    ```
    file:///Users/Joe/Portfiles
    ```

    Note the triple slashes and save the file. Now, MacPorts knows that it has to search for Portfiles in `<local_repository>` first, and then, its default online repository.

3. Open the terminal and update MacPorts to ensure that we have the latest Portfiles from the default repository:

    ```
    $ sudo port selfupdate
    ```

4. Let's copy the default repository's `opencv` Portfile as an example. We should also copy the directory structure, which determines how the package is categorized by MacPorts:

```
$ mkdir <local_repository>/graphics/
```

```
$ cp /opt/local/var/macports/sources/rsync.macports.org/release/
ports/graphics/opencv <local_repository>/graphics
```

Alternatively, for an example that includes Kinect support, we could download my online repository from `http://nummist.com/opencv/ports.tar.gz`, unzip it, and copy its entire `graphics` folder into `<local_repository>`:

```
$ cp <unzip_destination>/graphics <local_repository>
```

5. Edit `<local_repository>/graphics/opencv/Portfile`. Note that this file specifies the CMake configuration flags, dependencies, and variants. For details on the Portfile editing, go to `http://guide.macports.org/#development`.

To see which CMake configuration flags are relevant to OpenCV, we need to look at its source code. Download the source code archive from `https://github.com/Itseez/opencv/archive/3.0.0.zip`, unzip it to any location, and read `<unzip_destination>/OpenCV-3.0.0/CMakeLists.txt`.

After making any edits to the Portfile, save it.

6. Now, we need to generate an index file in our local repository so that MacPorts can find the new Portfile:

```
$ cd <local_repository>
```

```
$ portindex
```

7. From now on, we can treat our custom `opencv` file just like any other MacPorts package. For example, we can install it as follows:

```
$ sudo port install opencv +python27 +openni_sensorkinect
```

Note that our local repository's Portfile takes precedence over the default repository's Portfile because of the order in which they are listed in `/opt/local/etc/macports/sources.conf`.

Using Homebrew with ready-made packages (no support for depth cameras)

Homebrew is another package manager that can help us. Normally, MacPorts and Homebrew should not be installed on the same machine.

Starting from a system where Xcode and its command-line tools are already set up, the following steps will give us an OpenCV installation via Homebrew:

1. Open the terminal and run the following command to install Homebrew:

   ```
   $ ruby -e "$(curl -fsSkLraw.github.com/mxcl/homebrew/go)"
   ```

2. Unlike MacPorts, Homebrew does not automatically put its executables in PATH. To do so, create or edit the ~/.profile file and add this line at the top of the code:

   ```
   export PATH=/usr/local/bin:/usr/local/sbin:$PATH
   ```

   Save the file and run this command to refresh PATH:

   ```
   $ source ~/.profile
   ```

   Note that executables installed by Homebrew now take precedence over executables installed by the system.

3. For Homebrew's self-diagnostic report, run the following command:

   ```
   $ brew doctor
   ```

   Follow any troubleshooting advice it gives.

4. Now, update Homebrew:

   ```
   $ brew update
   ```

5. Run the following command to install Python 2.7:

   ```
   $ brew install python
   ```

6. Now, we can install NumPy. Homebrew's selection of the Python library packages is limited, so we use a separate package management tool called pip, which comes with Homebrew's Python:

   ```
   $ pip install numpy
   ```

7. SciPy contains some Fortran code, so we need an appropriate compiler. We can use Homebrew to install the gfortran compiler:

   ```
   $ brew install gfortran
   ```

   Now, we can install SciPy:

   ```
   $ pip install scipy
   ```

8. To install OpenCV on a 64-bit system (all new Mac hardware since late 2006), run the following command:

```
$ brew install opencv
```

Downloading the example code

You can download the example code files for all Packt Publishing books that you have purchased from your account at http://www.packtpub.com. If you purchased this book elsewhere, you can visit http://www.packtpub.com/support and register to have the files e-mailed directly to you.

Using Homebrew with your own custom packages

Homebrew makes it easy to edit existing package definitions:

```
$ brew edit opencv
```

The package definitions are actually scripts in the Ruby programming language. Tips on editing them can be found on the Homebrew Wiki page at https://github.com/mxcl/homebrew/wiki/Formula-Cookbook. A script may specify Make or CMake configuration flags, among other things.

To see which CMake configuration flags are relevant to OpenCV, we need to look at its source code. Download the source code archive from https://github.com/Itseez/opencv/archive/3.0.0.zip, unzip it to any location, and read <unzip_destination>/OpenCV-2.4.3/CMakeLists.txt.

After making edits to the Ruby script, save it.

The customized package can be treated as normal. For example, it can be installed as follows:

```
$ brew install opencv
```

Installation on Ubuntu and its derivatives

First and foremost, here is a quick note on Ubuntu's versions of an operating system: Ubuntu has a 6-month release cycle in which each release is either a .04 or a .10 minor version of a major version (14 at the time of writing). Every two years, however, Ubuntu releases a version classified as **long-term support** (**LTS**) which will grant you a five year support by Canonical (the company behind Ubuntu). If you work in an enterprise environment, it is certainly advisable to install one of the LTS versions. The latest one available is 14.04.

Ubuntu comes with Python 2.7 preinstalled. The standard Ubuntu repository contains OpenCV 2.4.9 packages without support for depth cameras. At the time of writing this, OpenCV 3 is not yet available through the Ubuntu repositories, so we will have to build it from source. Fortunately, the vast majority of Unix-like and Linux systems come with all the necessary software to build a project from scratch already installed. When built from source, OpenCV can support depth cameras via OpenNI and SensorKinect, which are available as precompiled binaries with installation scripts.

Using the Ubuntu repository (no support for depth cameras)

We can install Python and all its necessary dependencies using the `apt` package manager, by running the following commands:

```
> sudo apt-get install build-essential
```

```
> sudo apt-get install cmake git libgtk2.0-dev pkg-config libavcodecdev libavformat-dev libswscale-dev
```

```
> sudo apt-get install python-dev python-numpy libtbb2 libtbb-dev libjpeg-dev libpng-dev libtiff-dev libjasper-dev libdc1394-22-dev
```

Equivalently, we could have used Ubuntu Software Center, which is the `apt` package manager's graphical frontend.

Building OpenCV from a source

Now that we have the entire Python stack and `cmake` installed, we can build OpenCV. First, we need to download the source code from `https://github.com/Itseez/opencv/archive/3.0.0-beta.zip`.

Extract the archive and move it into the unzipped folder in a terminal.

Then, run the following commands:

```
> mkdir build
```

```
> cd build
```

```
> cmake -D CMAKE_BUILD_TYPE=Release -D CMAKE_INSTALL_PREFIX=/usr/local ..
```

```
> make
```

```
> make install
```

After the installation terminates, you might want to look at OpenCV's Python samples in `<opencv_folder>/opencv/samples/python` and `<script_folder>/opencv/samples/python2`.

Installation on other Unix-like systems

The approaches for Ubuntu (as described previously) are likely to work on any Linux distribution derived from Ubuntu 14.04 LTS or Ubuntu 14.10 as follows:

- Kubuntu 14.04 LTS or Kubuntu 14.10
- Xubuntu 14.04 LTS or Xubuntu 14.10
- Linux Mint 17

On Debian Linux and its derivatives, the `apt` package manager works the same as on Ubuntu, though the available packages may differ.

On Gentoo Linux and its derivatives, the Portage package manager is similar to MacPorts (as described previously), though the available packages may differ.

On FreeBSD derivatives, the process of installation is again similar to MacPorts; in fact, MacPorts derives from the `ports` installation system adopted on FreeBSD. Consult the remarkable FreeBSD Handbook at `https://www.freebsd.org/doc/handbook/` for an overview of the software installation process.

On other Unix-like systems, the package manager and available packages may differ. Consult your package manager's documentation and search for packages with `opencv` in their names. Remember that OpenCV and its Python bindings might be split into multiple packages.

Also, look for any installation notes published by the system provider, the repository maintainer, or the community. Since OpenCV uses camera drivers and media codecs, getting all of its functionality to work can be tricky on systems with poor multimedia support. Under some circumstances, system packages might need to be reconfigured or reinstalled for compatibility.

If packages are available for OpenCV, check their version number. OpenCV 3 or higher is recommended for this book's purposes. Also, check whether the packages offer Python bindings and depth camera support via OpenNI and SensorKinect. Finally, check whether anyone in the developer community has reported success or failure in using the packages.

If, instead, we want to do a custom build of OpenCV from source, it might be helpful to refer to the installation script for Ubuntu (as discussed previously) and adapt it to the package manager and packages that are present on another system.

Installing the Contrib modules

Unlike with OpenCV 2.4, some modules are contained in a repository called `opencv_contrib`, which is available at `https://github.com/Itseez/opencv_contrib`. I highly recommend installing these modules as they contain extra functionalities that are not included in OpenCV, such as the face recognition module.

Once downloaded (either through `zip` or `git`, I recommend `git` so that you can keep up to date with a simple `git pull` command), you can rerun your `cmake` command to include the building of OpenCV with the `opencv_contrib` modules as follows:

```
cmake -DOPENCV_EXTRA_MODULES_PATH=<opencv_contrib>/modules <opencv_
source_directory>
```

So, if you've followed the standard procedure and created a build directory in your OpenCV download folder, you should run the following command:

```
mkdir build && cd build
```

```
cmake -D CMAKE_BUILD_TYPE=Release -DOPENCV_EXTRA_MODULES_PATH=<opencv_
contrib>/modules  -D CMAKE_INSTALL_PREFIX=/usr/local ..
```

```
make
```

Running samples

Running a few sample scripts is a good way to test whether OpenCV is correctly set up. The samples are included in OpenCV's source code archive.

On Windows, we should have already downloaded and unzipped OpenCV's self-extracting ZIP. Find the samples in `<unzip_destination>/opencv/samples`.

On Unix-like systems, including Mac, download the source code archive from `https://github.com/Itseez/opencv/archive/3.0.0.zip` and unzip it to any location (if we have not already done so). Find the samples in `<unzip_destination>/OpenCV-3.0.0/samples`.

Some of the sample scripts require command-line arguments. However, the following scripts (among others) should work without any arguments:

- `python/camera.py`: This script displays a webcam feed (assuming that a webcam is plugged in).

- `python/drawing.py`: This script draws a series of shapes, such as a screensaver.

- `python2/hist.py`: This script displays a photo. Press *A*, *B*, *C*, *D*, or *E* to see the variations of the photo along with a corresponding histogram of color or grayscale values.

- `python2/opt_flow.py` (missing from the Ubuntu package): This script displays a webcam feed with a superimposed visualization of an optical flow (such as the direction of motion). For example, slowly wave your hand at the webcam to see the effect. Press *1* or *2* for alternative visualizations.

To exit a script, press *Esc* (not the window's close button).

If we encounter the `ImportError: No module` named `cv2.cv` message, then this means that we are running the script from a Python installation that does not know anything about OpenCV. There are two possible explanations for this:

- Some steps in the OpenCV installation might have failed or been missed. Go back and review the steps.

- If we have multiple Python installations on the machine, we might be using the wrong version of Python to launch the script. For example, on Mac, it might be the case that OpenCV is installed for MacPorts Python, but we are running the script with the system's Python. Go back and review the installation steps about editing the system path. Also, try launching the script manually from the command line using commands such as this:

  ```
  $ python python/camera.py
  ```

  You can also use the following command:

  ```
  $ python2.7 python/camera.py
  ```

  As another possible means of selecting a different Python installation, try editing the sample script to remove the `#!` lines. These lines might explicitly associate the script with the wrong Python installation (for our particular setup).

Finding documentation, help, and updates

OpenCV's documentation can be found online at http://docs.opencv.org/. The documentation includes a combined API reference for OpenCV's new C++ API, its new Python API (which is based on the C++ API), old C API, and its old Python API (which is based on the C API). When looking up a class or function, be sure to read the section about the new Python API (the cv2 module), and not the old Python API (the cv module).

The documentation is also available as several downloadable PDF files:

- **API reference**: This documentation can be found at http://docs.opencv. org/modules/refman.html
- **Tutorials**: These documents can be found at http://docs.opencv.org/ doc/tutorials/tutorials.html (these tutorials use the C++ code; for a Python port of the tutorials' code, see the repository of Abid Rahman K. at http://goo.gl/EPsD1)

If you write code on airplanes or other places without Internet access, you will definitely want to keep offline copies of the documentation.

If the documentation does not seem to answer your questions, try talking to the OpenCV community. Here are some sites where you will find helpful people:

- **The OpenCV forum**: http://www.answers.opencv.org/questions/
- **David Millán Escrivá's blog** (one of this book's reviewers): http://blog. damiles.com/
- **Abid Rahman K.'s blog** (one of this book's reviewers): http://www. opencvpython.blogspot.com/
- **Adrian Rosebrock's website** (one of this book's reviewers): http://www. pyimagesearch.com/
- **Joe Minichino's website for this book** (author of this book): http:// techfort.github.io/pycv/
- **Joe Howse's website for this book** (author of the first edition of this book): http://nummist.com/opencv/

Lastly, if you are an advanced user who wants to try new features, bug fixes, and sample scripts from the latest (unstable) OpenCV source code, have a look at the project's repository at https://github.com/Itseez/opencv/.

Summary

By now, we should have an OpenCV installation that can do everything we need for the project described in this book. Depending on which approach we took, we might also have a set of tools and scripts that are usable to reconfigure and rebuild OpenCV for our future needs.

We know where to find OpenCV's Python samples. These samples covered a different range of functionalities outside this book's scope, but they are useful as additional learning aids.

In the next chapter, we will familiarize ourselves with the most basic functions of the OpenCV API, namely, displaying images, videos, capturing videos through a webcam, and handling basic keyboard and mouse inputs.

2
Handling Files, Cameras, and GUIs

Installing OpenCV and running samples is fun, but at this stage, we want to try it out ourselves. This chapter introduces OpenCV's I/O functionality. We also discuss the concept of a project and the beginnings of an object-oriented design for this project, which we will flesh out in subsequent chapters.

By starting with a look at the I/O capabilities and design patterns, we will build our project in the same way we would make a sandwich: from the outside in. Bread slices and spread, or endpoints and glue, come before fillings or algorithms. We choose this approach because computer vision is mostly extroverted—it contemplates the real world outside our computer—and we want to apply all our subsequent algorithmic work to the real world through a common interface.

Basic I/O scripts

Most CV applications need to get images as input. Most also produce images as output. An interactive CV application might require a camera as an input source and a window as an output destination. However, other possible sources and destinations include image files, video files, and raw bytes. For example, raw bytes might be transmitted via a network connection, or they might be generated by an algorithm if we incorporate procedural graphics into our application. Let's look at each of these possibilities.

Reading/writing an image file

OpenCV provides the `imread()` and `imwrite()` functions that support various file formats for still images. The supported formats vary by system but should always include the BMP format. Typically, PNG, JPEG, and TIFF should be among the supported formats too.

Let's explore the anatomy of the representation of an image in Python and NumPy.

No matter the format, each pixel has a value, but the difference is in how the pixel is represented. For example, we can create a black square image from scratch by simply creating a 2D NumPy array:

```
img = numpy.zeros((3,3), dtype=numpy.uint8)
```

If we print this image to a console, we obtain the following result:

```
array([[0, 0, 0],
       [0, 0, 0],
       [0, 0, 0]], dtype=uint8)
```

Each pixel is represented by a single 8-bit integer, which means that the values for each pixel are in the 0-255 range.

Let's now convert this image into **Blue-green-red (BGR)** using `cv2.cvtColor`:

```
img = cv2.cvtColor(img, cv2.COLOR_GRAY2BGR)
```

Let's observe how the image has changed:

```
array([[[0, 0, 0],
        [0, 0, 0],
        [0, 0, 0]],

       [[0, 0, 0],
        [0, 0, 0],
        [0, 0, 0]],

       [[0, 0, 0],
        [0, 0, 0],
        [0, 0, 0]]], dtype=uint8)
```

As you can see, each pixel is now represented by a three-element array, with each integer representing the B, G, and R channels, respectively. Other color spaces, such as HSV, will be represented in the same way, albeit with different value ranges (for example, the hue value of the HSV color space has a range of 0-180) and different numbers of channels.

You can check the structure of an image by inspecting the `shape` property, which returns rows, columns, and the number of channels (if there is more than one).

Consider this example:

```
>>> img = numpy.zeros((3,3), dtype=numpy.uint8)
>>> img.shape
```

The preceding code will print `(3,3)`. If you then converted the image to BGR, the shape would be `(3,3,3)`, which indicates the presence of three channels per pixel.

Images can be loaded from one file format and saved to another. For example, let's convert an image from PNG to JPEG:

```
import cv2

image = cv2.imread('MyPic.png')
cv2.imwrite('MyPic.jpg', image)
```

 Most of the OpenCV functionalities that we use are in the `cv2` module. You might come across other OpenCV guides that instead rely on the `cv` or `cv2.cv` modules, which are legacy versions. The reason why the Python module is called `cv2` is not because it is a Python binding module for OpenCV 2.x.x, but because it has introduced a better API, which leverages object-oriented programming as opposed to the previous `cv` module, which adhered to a more procedural style of programming.

By default, `imread()` returns an image in the BGR color format even if the file uses a grayscale format. BGR represents the same color space as **red-green-blue (RGB)**, but the byte order is reversed.

Optionally, we may specify the mode of `imread()` to be one of the following enumerators:

- `IMREAD_ANYCOLOR = 4`
- `IMREAD_ANYDEPTH = 2`
- `IMREAD_COLOR = 1`
- `IMREAD_GRAYSCALE = 0`
- `IMREAD_LOAD_GDAL = 8`
- `IMREAD_UNCHANGED = -1`

For example, let's load a PNG file as a grayscale image (losing any color information in the process), and then, save it as a grayscale PNG image:

```
import cv2

grayImage = cv2.imread('MyPic.png', cv2.IMREAD_GRAYSCALE)
cv2.imwrite('MyPicGray.png', grayImage)
```

To avoid unnecessary headaches, use absolute paths to your images (for example, C:\Users\Joe\Pictures\MyPic.png on Windows or /home/joe/pictures/MyPic.png on Unix) at least while you're familiarizing yourself with OpenCV's API. The path of an image, unless absolute, is relative to the folder that contains the Python script, so in the preceding example, MyPic.png would have to be in the same folder as your Python script or the image won't be found.

Regardless of the mode, imread() discards any alpha channel (transparency). The imwrite() function requires an image to be in the BGR or grayscale format with a certain number of bits per channel that the output format can support. For example, bmp requires 8 bits per channel, while PNG allows either 8 or 16 bits per channel.

Converting between an image and raw bytes

Conceptually, a byte is an integer ranging from 0 to 255. In all real-time graphic applications today, a pixel is typically represented by one byte per channel, though other representations are also possible.

An OpenCV image is a 2D or 3D array of the .array type. An 8-bit grayscale image is a 2D array containing byte values. A 24-bit BGR image is a 3D array, which also contains byte values. We may access these values by using an expression, such as image[0, 0] or image[0, 0, 0]. The first index is the pixel's *y* coordinate or row, 0 being the top. The second index is the pixel's *x* coordinate or column, 0 being the leftmost. The third index (if applicable) represents a color channel.

For example, in an 8-bit grayscale image with a white pixel in the upper-left corner, image[0, 0] is 255. For a 24-bit BGR image with a blue pixel in the upper-left corner, image[0, 0] is [255, 0, 0].

As an alternative to using an expression, such as image[0, 0] or image[0, 0] = 128, we may use an expression, such as image.item((0, 0)) or image.setitem((0, 0), 128). The latter expressions are more efficient for single-pixel operations. However, as we will see in subsequent chapters, we usually want to perform operations on large slices of an image rather than on single pixels.

Provided that an image has 8 bits per channel, we can cast it to a standard Python `bytearray`, which is one-dimensional:

```
byteArray = bytearray(image)
```

Conversely, provided that `bytearray` contains bytes in an appropriate order, we can cast and then reshape it to get a `numpy.array` type that is an image:

```
grayImage = numpy.array(grayByteArray).reshape(height, width)
bgrImage = numpy.array(bgrByteArray).reshape(height, width, 3)
```

As a more complete example, let's convert `bytearray`, which contains random bytes to a grayscale image and a BGR image:

```
import cv2
import numpy
import os

# Make an array of 120,000 random bytes.
randomByteArray = bytearray(os.urandom(120000))
flatNumpyArray = numpy.array(randomByteArray)

# Convert the array to make a 400x300 grayscale image.
grayImage = flatNumpyArray.reshape(300, 400)
cv2.imwrite('RandomGray.png', grayImage)

# Convert the array to make a 400x100 color image.
bgrImage = flatNumpyArray.reshape(100, 400, 3)
cv2.imwrite('RandomColor.png', bgrImage)
```

After running this script, we should have a pair of randomly generated images, `RandomGray.png` and `RandomColor.png`, in the script's directory.

 Here, we use Python's standard `os.urandom()` function to generate random raw bytes, which we will then convert to a NumPy array. Note that it is also possible to generate a random NumPy array directly (and more efficiently) using a statement, such as `numpy.random.randint(0, 256, 120000).reshape(300, 400)`. The only reason we use `os.urandom()` is to help demonstrate a conversion from raw bytes.

Accessing image data with numpy.array

Now that you have a better understanding of how an image is formed, we can start performing basic operations on it. We know that the easiest (and most common) way to load an image in OpenCV is to use the `imread` function. We also know that this will return an image, which is really an array (either a 2D or 3D one, depending on the parameters you passed to `imread()`).

The `y.array` structure is well optimized for array operations, and it allows certain kinds of bulk manipulations that are not available in a plain Python list. These kinds of `.array` type-specific operations come in handy for image manipulations in OpenCV. Let's explore image manipulations from the start and step by step though, with a basic example: say you want to manipulate a pixel at the coordinates, (0, 0), of a BGR image and turn it into a white pixel.

```
import cv

import numpy as np
img = cv.imread('MyPic.png')
img[0,0] = [255, 255, 255]
```

If you then showed the image with a standard `imshow()` call, you will see a white dot in the top-left corner of the image. Naturally, this isn't very useful, but it shows what can be accomplished. Let's now leverage the ability of `numpy.array` to operate transformations to an array much faster than a plain Python array.

Let's say that you want to change the blue value of a particular pixel, for example, the pixel at coordinates, (150, 120). The `numpy.array` type provides a very handy method, `item()`, which takes three parameters: the x (or left) position, y (or top), and the index within the array at (x, y) position (remember that in a BGR image, the data at a certain position is a three-element array containing the B, G, and R values in this order) and returns the value at the index position. Another `itemset()` method sets the value of a particular channel of a particular pixel to a specified value (`itemset()` takes two arguments: a three-element tuple (x, y, and index) and the new value).

In this example, we will change the value of blue at (150, 120) from its current value (127) to an arbitrary 255:

```
import cv
import numpy as  np
img = cv.imread('MyPic.png')
print img.item(150, 120, 0)   // prints the current value of B for that
pixel
img.itemset( (150, 120, 0), 255)
print img.item(150, 120, 0)   // prints 255
```

Remember that we do this with `numpy.array` for two reasons: `numpy.array` is an extremely optimized library for these kind of operations, and because we obtain more readable code through NumPy's elegant methods rather than the raw index access of the first example.

This particular code doesn't do much in itself, but it does open a world of possibilities. It is, however, advisable that you utilize built-in filters and methods to manipulate an entire image; the above approach is only suitable for small regions of interest.

Now, let's take a look at a very common operation, namely, manipulating channels. Sometimes, you'll want to zero-out all the values of a particular channel (B, G, or R).

Using loops to manipulate the Python arrays is very costly in terms of runtime and should be avoided at all costs. Using array indexing allows for efficient manipulation of pixels. This is a costly and slow operation, especially if you manipulate videos, you'll find yourself with a jittery output. Then a feature called indexing comes to the rescue. Setting all G (green) values of an image to 0 is as simple as using this code:

```
import cv
import as np
img = cv.imread('MyPic.png')
img[:, :, 1] = 0
```

This is a fairly impressive piece of code and easy to understand. The relevant line is the last one, which basically instructs the program to take all pixels from all rows and columns and set the resulting value at index one of the three-element array, representing the color of the pixel to 0. If you display this image, you will notice a complete absence of green.

There are a number of interesting things we can do by accessing raw pixels with NumPy's array indexing; one of them is defining **regions of interests** (**ROI**). Once the region is defined, we can perform a number of operations, namely, binding this region to a variable, and then even defining a second region and assigning it the value of the first one (visually copying a portion of the image over to another position in the image):

```
import cv
import numpy as np
img = cv.imread('MyPic.png')
my_roi = img[0:100, 0:100]
img[300:400, 300:400] = my_roi
```

It's important to make sure that the two regions correspond in terms of size. If not, NumPy will (rightly) complain that the two shapes mismatch.

Finally, there are a few interesting details we can obtain from `numpy.array`, such as the image properties using this code:

```
import cv
import numpy  as  np
img = cv.imread('MyPic.png')
print img.shape
print img.size
print img.dtype
```

These three properties are in this order:

- **Shape**: NumPy returns a tuple containing the width, height, and—if the image is in color—the number of channels. This is useful to debug a type of image; if the image is monochromatic or grayscale, it will not contain a channel's value.
- **Size**: This property refers to the size of an image in pixels.
- **Datatype**: This property refers to the datatype used for an image (normally a variation of an unsigned integer type and the bits supported by this type, that is, `uint8`).

All in all, it is strongly advisable that you familiarize yourself with NumPy in general and `numpy.array` in particular when working with OpenCV, as it is the foundation of an image processing done with Python.

Reading/writing a video file

OpenCV provides the `VideoCapture` and `VideoWriter` classes that support various video file formats. The supported formats vary by system but should always include an AVI. Via its `read()` method, a `VideoCapture` class may be polled for new frames until it reaches the end of its video file. Each frame is an image in a BGR format.

Conversely, an image may be passed to the `write()` method of the `VideoWriter` class, which appends the image to a file in `VideoWriter`. Let's look at an example that reads frames from one AVI file and writes them to another with a YUV encoding:

```
import cv2

videoCapture = cv2.VideoCapture('MyInputVid.avi')
fps = videoCapture.get(cv2.CAP_PROP_FPS)
size = (int(videoCapture.get(cv2.CAP_PROP_FRAME_WIDTH)),
```

```
            int(videoCapture.get(cv2.CAP_PROP_FRAME_HEIGHT)))
videoWriter = cv2.VideoWriter(
    'MyOutputVid.avi', cv2.VideoWriter_fourcc('I','4','2','0'),
        fps, size)

success, frame = videoCapture.read()
while success: # Loop until there are no more frames.
    videoWriter.write(frame)
    success, frame = videoCapture.read()
```

The arguments to the `VideoWriter` class constructor deserve special attention. A video's filename must be specified. Any preexisting file with this name is overwritten. A video codec must also be specified. The available codecs may vary from system to system. These are the options that are included:

- `cv2.VideoWriter_fourcc('I','4','2','0')`: This option is an uncompressed YUV encoding, 4:2:0 chroma subsampled. This encoding is widely compatible but produces large files. The file extension should be `.avi`.

- `cv2.VideoWriter_fourcc('P','I','M','1')`: This option is MPEG-1. The file extension should be `.avi`.

- `cv2.VideoWriter_fourcc('X','V','I','D')`: This option is MPEG-4 and a preferred option if you want the resulting video size to be average. The file extension should be `.avi`.

- `cv2.VideoWriter_fourcc('T','H','E','O')`: This option is Ogg Vorbis. The file extension should be `.ogv`.

- `cv2.VideoWriter_fourcc('F','L','V','1')`: This option is a Flash video. The file extension should be `.flv`.

A frame rate and frame size must be specified too. Since we are copying video frames from another video, these properties can be read from the `get()` method of the `VideoCapture` class.

Capturing camera frames

A stream of camera frames is represented by the `VideoCapture` class too. However, for a camera, we construct a `VideoCapture` class by passing the camera's device index instead of a video's filename. Let's consider an example that captures 10 seconds of video from a camera and writes it to an AVI file:

```
import cv2

cameraCapture = cv2.VideoCapture(0)
fps = 30 # an assumption
```

```
size = (int(cameraCapture.get(cv2.CAP_PROP_FRAME_WIDTH)),
        int(cameraCapture.get(cv2.CAP_PROP_FRAME_HEIGHT)))
videoWriter = cv2.VideoWriter(
    'MyOutputVid.avi', cv2.VideoWriter_fourcc('I','4','2','0'),
      fps, size)

success, frame = cameraCapture.read()
numFramesRemaining = 10 * fps - 1
while success and numFramesRemaining > 0:
    videoWriter.write(frame)
    success, frame = cameraCapture.read()
    numFramesRemaining -= 1
cameraCapture.release()
```

Unfortunately, the `get()` method of a `VideoCapture` class does not return an accurate value for the camera's frame rate; it always returns `0`. The official documentation at `http://docs.opencv.org/modules/highgui/doc/reading_ and_writing_images_and_video.html` reads:

> *"When querying a property that is not supported by the backend used by the `VideoCapture` class, value 0 is returned."*

This occurs most commonly on systems where the driver only supports basic functionalities.

For the purpose of creating an appropriate `VideoWriter` class for the camera, we have to either make an assumption about the frame rate (as we did in the code previously) or measure it using a timer. The latter approach is better and we will cover it later in this chapter.

The number of cameras and their order is of course system-dependent. Unfortunately, OpenCV does not provide any means of querying the number of cameras or their properties. If an invalid index is used to construct a `VideoCapture` class, the `VideoCapture` class will not yield any frames; its `read()` method will return `(false, None)`. A good way to prevent it from trying to retrieve frames from `VideoCapture` that were not opened correctly is to use the `VideoCapture.isOpened` method, which returns a Boolean.

The `read()` method is inappropriate when we need to synchronize a set of cameras or a multihead camera (such as a stereo camera or Kinect). Then, we use the `grab()` and `retrieve()` methods instead. For a set of cameras, we use this code:

```
success0 = cameraCapture0.grab()
success1 = cameraCapture1.grab()
if success0 and success1:
    frame0 = cameraCapture0.retrieve()
    frame1 = cameraCapture1.retrieve()
```

Displaying images in a window

One of the most basic operations in OpenCV is displaying an image. This can be done with the `imshow()` function. If you come from any other GUI framework background, you would think it sufficient to call `imshow()` to display an image. This is only partially true: the image will be displayed, and will disappear immediately. This is by design, to enable the constant refreshing of a window frame when working with videos. Here's a very simple example code to display an image:

```
import cv2
import numpy as np

img = cv2.imread('my-image.png')
cv2.imshow('my image', img)
cv2.waitKey()
cv2.destroyAllWindows()
```

The `imshow()` function takes two parameters: the name of the frame in which we want to display the image, and the image itself. We'll talk about `waitKey()` in more detail when we explore the displaying of frames in a window.

The aptly named `destroyAllWindows()` function disposes of all the windows created by OpenCV.

Displaying camera frames in a window

OpenCV allows named windows to be created, redrawn, and destroyed using the `namedWindow()`, `imshow()`, and `destroyWindow()` functions. Also, any window may capture keyboard input via the `waitKey()` function and mouse input via the `setMouseCallback()` function. Let's look at an example where we show the frames of a live camera input:

```python
import cv2

clicked = False
def onMouse(event, x, y, flags, param):
    global clicked
    if event == cv2.EVENT_LBUTTONUP:
        clicked = True

cameraCapture = cv2.VideoCapture(0)
cv2.namedWindow('MyWindow')
cv2.setMouseCallback('MyWindow', onMouse)

print 'Showing camera feed. Click window or press any key to
    stop.'
success, frame = cameraCapture.read()
while success and cv2.waitKey(1) == -1 and not clicked:
    cv2.imshow('MyWindow', frame)
    success, frame = cameraCapture.read()

cv2.destroyWindow('MyWindow')
cameraCapture.release()
```

The argument for `waitKey()` is a number of milliseconds to wait for keyboard input. The return value is either -1 (meaning that no key has been pressed) or an ASCII keycode, such as 27 for *Esc*. For a list of ASCII keycodes, see `http://www.asciitable.com/`. Also, note that Python provides a standard function, `ord()`, which can convert a character to its ASCII keycode. For example, `ord('a')` returns 97.

> On some systems, `waitKey()` may return a value that encodes more than just the ASCII keycode. (A bug is known to occur on Linux when OpenCV uses GTK as its backend GUI library.) On all systems, we can ensure that we extract just the ASCII keycode by reading the last byte from the return value like this:
>
> ```python
> keycode = cv2.waitKey(1)
> if keycode != -1:
>     keycode &= 0xFF
> ```

OpenCV's window functions and `waitKey()` are interdependent. OpenCV windows are only updated when `waitKey()` is called, and `waitKey()` only captures input when an OpenCV window has focus.

The mouse callback passed to `setMouseCallback()` should take five arguments, as seen in our code sample. The callback's `param` argument is set as an optional third argument to `setMouseCallback()`. By default, it is 0. The callback's event argument is one of the following actions:

- `cv2.EVENT_MOUSEMOVE`: This event refers to mouse movement
- `cv2.EVENT_LBUTTONDOWN`: This event refers to the left button down
- `cv2.EVENT_RBUTTONDOWN`: This refers to the right button down
- `cv2.EVENT_MBUTTONDOWN`: This refers to the middle button down
- `cv2.EVENT_LBUTTONUP`: This refers to the left button up
- `cv2.EVENT_RBUTTONUP`: This event refers to the right button up
- `cv2.EVENT_MBUTTONUP`: This event refers to the middle button up
- `cv2.EVENT_LBUTTONDBLCLK`: This event refers to the left button being double-clicked
- `cv2.EVENT_RBUTTONDBLCLK`: This refers to the right button being double-clicked
- `cv2.EVENT_MBUTTONDBLCLK`: This refers to the middle button being double-clicked

The mouse callback's flags argument may be some bitwise combination of the following events:

- `cv2.EVENT_FLAG_LBUTTON`: This event refers to the left button being pressed
- `cv2.EVENT_FLAG_RBUTTON`: This event refers to the right button being pressed
- `cv2.EVENT_FLAG_MBUTTON`: This event refers to the middle button being pressed
- `cv2.EVENT_FLAG_CTRLKEY`: This event refers to the *Ctrl* key being pressed
- `cv2.EVENT_FLAG_SHIFTKEY`: This event refers to the *Shift* key being pressed
- `cv2.EVENT_FLAG_ALTKEY`: This event refers to the *Alt* key being pressed

Unfortunately, OpenCV does not provide any means of handling window events. For example, we cannot stop our application when a window's close button is clicked. Due to OpenCV's limited event handling and GUI capabilities, many developers prefer to integrate it with other application frameworks. Later in this chapter, we will design an abstraction layer to help integrate OpenCV into any application framework.

Project Cameo (face tracking and image manipulation)

OpenCV is often studied through a cookbook approach that covers a lot of algorithms but nothing about high-level application development. To an extent, this approach is understandable because OpenCV's potential applications are so diverse. OpenCV is used in a wide variety of applications: photo/video editors, motion-controlled games, a robot's AI, or psychology experiments where we log participants' eye movements. Across such different use cases, can we truly study a useful set of abstractions?

I believe we can and the sooner we start creating abstractions, the better. We will structure our study of OpenCV around a single application, but, at each step, we will design a component of this application to be extensible and reusable.

We will develop an interactive application that performs face tracking and image manipulations on camera input in real time. This type of application covers a broad range of OpenCV's functionality and challenges us to create an efficient, effective implementation.

Specifically, our application will perform real-time facial merging. Given two streams of camera input (or, optionally, prerecorded video input), the application will superimpose faces from one stream onto faces in the other. Filters and distortions will be applied to give this blended scene a unified look and feel. Users should have the experience of being engaged in a live performance where they enter another environment and persona. This type of user experience is popular in amusement parks such as Disneyland.

In such an application, users would immediately notice flaws, such as a low frame rate or inaccurate tracking. To get the best results, we will try several approaches using conventional imaging and depth imaging.

We will call our application Cameo. A cameo is (in jewelry) a small portrait of a person or (in film) a very brief role played by a celebrity.

Cameo – an object-oriented design

Python applications can be written in a purely procedural style. This is often done with small applications, such as our basic I/O scripts, discussed previously. However, from now on, we will use an object-oriented style because it promotes modularity and extensibility.

From our overview of OpenCV's I/O functionality, we know that all images are similar, regardless of their source or destination. No matter how we obtain a stream of images or where we send it as output, we can apply the same application-specific logic to each frame in this stream. Separation of I/O code and application code becomes especially convenient in an application, such as Cameo, which uses multiple I/O streams.

We will create classes called `CaptureManager` and `WindowManager` as high-level interfaces to I/O streams. Our application code may use `CaptureManager` to read new frames and, optionally, to dispatch each frame to one or more outputs, including a still image file, a video file, and a window (via a `WindowManager` class). A `WindowManager` class lets our application code handle a window and events in an object-oriented style.

Both `CaptureManager` and `WindowManager` are extensible. We could make implementations that do not rely on OpenCV for I/O. Indeed, *Appendix A*, *Integrating with Pygame*, uses a `WindowManager` subclass.

Abstracting a video stream with managers. CaptureManager

As we have seen, OpenCV can capture, show, and record a stream of images from either a video file or a camera, but there are some special considerations in each case. Our `CaptureManager` class abstracts some of the differences and provides a higher-level interface to dispatch images from the capture stream to one or more outputs—a still image file, video file, or a window.

A `CaptureManager` class is initialized with a `VideoCapture` class and has the `enterFrame()` and `exitFrame()` methods that should typically be called on every iteration of an application's main loop. Between a call to `enterFrame()` and `exitFrame()`, the application may (any number of times) set a `channel` property and get a `frame` property. The `channel` property is initially 0 and only multihead cameras use other values. The `frame` property is an image corresponding to the current channel's state when `enterFrame()` was called.

A `CaptureManager` class also has the `writeImage()`, `startWritingVideo()`, and `stopWritingVideo()` methods that may be called at any time. Actual file writing is postponed until `exitFrame()`. Also, during the `exitFrame()` method, the `frame` property may be shown in a window, depending on whether the application code provides a `WindowManager` class either as an argument to the constructor of `CaptureManager` or by setting a `previewWindowManager` property.

If the application code manipulates `frame`, the manipulations are reflected in recorded files and in the window. A `CaptureManager` class has a constructor argument and property called `shouldMirrorPreview`, which should be `True` if we want `frame` to be mirrored (horizontally flipped) in the window but not in recorded files. Typically, when facing a camera, users prefer live camera feed to be mirrored.

Recall that a `VideoWriter` class needs a frame rate, but OpenCV does not provide any way to get an accurate frame rate for a camera. The `CaptureManager` class works around this limitation by using a frame counter and Python's standard `time.time()` function to estimate the frame rate if necessary. This approach is not foolproof. Depending on frame rate fluctuations and the system-dependent implementation of `time.time()`, the accuracy of the estimate might still be poor in some cases. However, if we deploy to unknown hardware, it is better than just assuming that the user's camera has a particular frame rate.

Let's create a file called `managers.py`, which will contain our implementation of `CaptureManager`. The implementation turns out to be quite long. So, we will look at it in several pieces. First, let's add imports, a constructor, and properties, as follows:

```python
import cv2
import numpy
import time

class CaptureManager(object):


    def __init__(self, capture, previewWindowManager = None,
                 shouldMirrorPreview = False):


        self.previewWindowManager = previewWindowManager
        self.shouldMirrorPreview = shouldMirrorPreview


        self._capture = capture
        self._channel = 0
        self._enteredFrame = False
        self._frame = None
```

```
        self._imageFilename = None
        self._videoFilename = None
        self._videoEncoding = None
        self._videoWriter = None

        self._startTime = None
        self._framesElapsed = long(0)
        self._fpsEstimate = None

    @property
    def channel(self):
        return self._channel

    @channel.setter
    def channel(self, value):
        if self._channel != value:
            self._channel = value
            self._frame = None

    @property
    def frame(self):
        if self._enteredFrame and self._frame is None:
            _, self._frame = self._capture.retrieve()
        return self._frame

    @property
    def isWritingImage (self):

        return self._imageFilename is not None

    @property
    def isWritingVideo(self):
        return self._videoFilename is not None
```

Note that most of the member variables are non-public, as denoted by the underscore prefix in variable names, such as self._enteredFrame. These nonpublic variables relate to the state of the current frame and any file-writing operations. As discussed previously, the application code only needs to configure a few things, which are implemented as constructor arguments and settable public properties: the camera channel, window manager, and the option to mirror the camera preview.

This book assumes a certain level of familiarity with Python; however, if you are getting confused by those @ annotations (for example, `@property`), refer to the Python documentation about `decorators`, a built-in feature of the language that allows the wrapping of a function by another function, normally used to apply a user-defined behavior in several places of an application (refer to `https://docs.python.org/2/reference/compound_stmts.html#grammar-token-decorator`).

> Python does not have the concept of private member variables and the single/double underscore prefix (_) is only a convention.
>
> By this convention, in Python, variables that are prefixed with a single underscore should be treated as protected (accessed only within the class and its subclasses), while variables that are prefixed with a double underscore should be treated as private (accessed only within the class).

Continuing with our implementation, let's add the `enterFrame()` and `exitFrame()` methods to `managers.py`:

```python
def enterFrame(self):
    """Capture the next frame, if any."""

    # But first, check that any previous frame was exited.
    assert not self._enteredFrame, \
        'previous enterFrame() had no matching exitFrame()'

    if self._capture is not None:
        self._enteredFrame = self._capture.grab()

def exitFrame (self):
    """Draw to the window. Write to files. Release the
        frame."""

    # Check whether any grabbed frame is retrievable.
    # The getter may retrieve and cache the frame.
    if self.frame is None:
        self._enteredFrame = False
        return

    # Update the FPS estimate and related variables.
    if self._framesElapsed == 0:
        self._startTime = time.time()
    else:
        timeElapsed = time.time() - self._startTime
```

```
            self._fpsEstimate = self._framesElapsed / timeElapsed
        self._framesElapsed += 1

        # Draw to the window, if any.
        if self.previewWindowManager is not None:
            if self.shouldMirrorPreview:
                mirroredFrame = numpy.fliplr(self._frame).copy()
                self.previewWindowManager.show(mirroredFrame)
            else:
                self.previewWindowManager.show(self._frame)

        # Write to the image file, if any.
        if self.isWritingImage:
            cv2.imwrite(self._imageFilename, self._frame)
            self._imageFilename = None

        # Write to the video file, if any.
        self._writeVideoFrame()

        # Release the frame.
        self._frame = None
        self._enteredFrame = False
```

Note that the implementation of enterFrame() only grabs (synchronizes) a frame, whereas actual retrieval from a channel is postponed to a subsequent reading of the frame variable. The implementation of exitFrame() takes the image from the current channel, estimates a frame rate, shows the image via the window manager (if any), and fulfills any pending requests to write the image to files.

Several other methods also pertain to file writing. To finish our class implementation, let's add the remaining file-writing methods to managers.py:

```
    def writeImage(self, filename):
        """Write the next exited frame to an image file."""
        self._imageFilename = filename

    def startWritingVideo(
            self, filename,
            encoding = cv2.VideoWriter_fourcc('I','4','2','0')):
        """Start writing exited frames to a video file."""
        self._videoFilename = filename
        self._videoEncoding = encoding

    def stopWritingVideo (self):
```

```
        """Stop writing exited frames to a video file."""
        self._videoFilename = None
        self._videoEncoding = None
        self._videoWriter = None


    def _writeVideoFrame(self):

        if not self.isWritingVideo:
            return

        if self._videoWriter is None:
            fps = self._capture.get(cv2.CAP_PROP_FPS)
            if fps == 0.0:
                # The capture's FPS is unknown so use an estimate.
                if self._framesElapsed < 20:
                    # Wait until more frames elapse so that the
                    # estimate is more stable.
                    return
                else:
                    fps = self._fpsEstimate
            size = (int(self._capture.get(
                        cv2.CAP_PROP_FRAME_WIDTH)),
                    int(self._capture.get(
                        cv2.CAP_PROP_FRAME_HEIGHT)))
            self._videoWriter = cv2.VideoWriter(
                self._videoFilename, self._videoEncoding,
                fps, size)

        self._videoWriter.write(self._frame)
```

The writeImage(), startWritingVideo(), and stopWritingVideo() public methods simply record the parameters for file-writing operations, whereas the actual writing operations are postponed to the next call of exitFrame(). The _writeVideoFrame() nonpublic method creates or appends a video file in a manner that should be familiar from our earlier scripts. (See the *Reading/writing a video file* section.) However, in situations where the frame rate is unknown, we skip some frames at the start of the capture session so that we have time to build up an estimate of the frame rate.

Although our current implementation of `CaptureManager` relies on `VideoCapture`, we could make other implementations that do not use OpenCV for input. For example, we could make a subclass that is instantiated with a socket connection, whose byte stream could be parsed as a stream of images. We could also make a subclass that uses a third-party camera library with different hardware support than what OpenCV provides. However, for Cameo, our current implementation is sufficient.

Abstracting a window and keyboard with managers.WindowManager

As we have seen, OpenCV provides functions that cause a window to be created, destroyed, show an image, and process events. Rather than being methods of a window class, these functions require a window's name to pass as an argument. Since this interface is not object-oriented, it is inconsistent with OpenCV's general style. Also, it is unlikely to be compatible with other window or event handling interfaces that we might eventually want to use instead of OpenCV's.

For the sake of object orientation and adaptability, we abstract this functionality into a `WindowManager` class with the `createWindow()`, `destroyWindow()`, `show()`, and `processEvents()` methods. As a property, a `WindowManager` class has a function object called `keypressCallback`, which (if not `None`) is called from `processEvents()` in response to any key press. The `keypressCallback` object must take a single argument, such as an ASCII keycode.

Let's add the following implementation of `WindowManager` to `managers.py`:

```
class WindowManager(object):


    def __init__(self, windowName, keypressCallback = None):
        self.keypressCallback = keypressCallback

        self._windowName = windowName
        self._isWindowCreated = False


    @property
    def isWindowCreated(self):
        return self._isWindowCreated

    def createWindow (self):
```

```
        cv2.namedWindow(self._windowName)
        self._isWindowCreated = True

    def show(self, frame):
        cv2.imshow(self._windowName, frame)

    def destroyWindow (self):
        cv2.destroyWindow(self._windowName)
        self._isWindowCreated = False

    def processEvents (self):
        keycode = cv2.waitKey(1)
        if self.keypressCallback is not None and keycode != -1:
            # Discard any non-ASCII info encoded by GTK.
            keycode &= 0xFF
            self.keypressCallback(keycode)
```

Our current implementation only supports keyboard events, which will be sufficient for Cameo. However, we could modify WindowManager to support mouse events too. For example, the class's interface could be expanded to include a mouseCallback property (and optional constructor argument), but could otherwise remain the same. With some event framework other than OpenCV's, we could support additional event types in the same way by adding callback properties.

Appendix A, Integrating with Pygame, shows a WindowManager subclass that is implemented with Pygame's window handling and event framework instead of OpenCV's. This implementation improves on the base WindowManager class by properly handling quit events—for example, when a user clicks on a window's close button. Potentially, many other event types can be handled via Pygame too.

Applying everything with cameo.Cameo

Our application is represented by a Cameo class with two methods: run() and onKeypress(). On initialization, a Cameo class creates a WindowManager class with onKeypress() as a callback, as well as a CaptureManager class using a camera and the WindowManager class. When run() is called, the application executes a main loop in which frames and events are processed. As a result of event processing, onKeypress() may be called. The spacebar causes a screenshot to be taken, *Tab* causes a screencast (a video recording) to start/stop, and *Esc* causes the application to quit.

In the same directory as `managers.py`, let's create a file called `cameo.py` containing the following implementation of `Cameo`:

```python
import cv2
from managers import WindowManager, CaptureManager

class Cameo(object):

    def __init__(self):
        self._windowManager = WindowManager('Cameo',
                                            self.onKeypress)
        self._captureManager = CaptureManager(
            cv2.VideoCapture(0), self._windowManager, True)

    def run(self):
        """Run the main loop."""
        self._windowManager.createWindow()
        while self._windowManager.isWindowCreated:
            self._captureManager.enterFrame()
            frame = self._captureManager.frame

            # TODO: Filter the frame (Chapter 3).

            self._captureManager.exitFrame()
            self._windowManager.processEvents()

    def onKeypress (self, keycode):
        """Handle a keypress.

        space   -> Take a screenshot.
        tab     -> Start/stop recording a screencast.
        escape -> Quit.

        """
        if keycode == 32: # space
            self._captureManager.writeImage('screenshot.png')
        elif keycode == 9: # tab
            if not self._captureManager.isWritingVideo:
                self._captureManager.startWritingVideo(
                    'screencast.avi')
            else:
                self._captureManager.stopWritingVideo()
        elif keycode == 27: # escape
            self._windowManager.destroyWindow()

if __name__=="__main__":
    Cameo().run()
```

When running the application, note that the live camera feed is mirrored, while screenshots and screencasts are not. This is the intended behavior, as we pass True for shouldMirrorPreview when initializing the CaptureManager class.

So far, we do not manipulate the frames in any way except to mirror them for preview. We will start to add more interesting effects in *Chapter 3, Filtering Images*.

Summary

By now, we should have an application that displays a camera feed, listens for keyboard input, and (on command) records a screenshot or screencast. We are ready to extend the application by inserting some image-filtering code (*Chapter 3, Filtering Images*) between the start and end of each frame. Optionally, we are also ready to integrate other camera drivers or application frameworks (*Appendix A, Integrating with Pygame*) besides the ones supported by OpenCV.

We also now have the knowledge to process images and understand the principle of image manipulation through the NumPy arrays. This forms the perfect foundation to understand the next topic, filtering images.

3
Processing Images with OpenCV 3

Sooner or later, when working with images, you will find yourself in need of altering images: be it applying artistic filters, extrapolating certain sections, cutting, pasting, or whatever else your mind can conjure. This chapter presents some techniques to alter images, and by the end of it, you should be able to perform tasks, such as detecting skin tone in an image, sharpening an image, mark contours of subjects, and detecting crosswalks using a line segment detector.

Converting between different color spaces

There are literally hundreds of methods in OpenCV that pertain to the conversion of color spaces. In general, three color spaces are prevalent in modern day computer vision: gray, BGR, and **Hue, Saturation, Value (HSV)**.

- Gray is a color space that effectively eliminates color information translating to shades of gray: this color space is extremely useful for intermediate processing, such as face detection.

- BGR is the blue-green-red color space, in which each pixel is a three-element array, each value representing the blue, green, and red colors: web developers would be familiar with a similar definition of colors, except the order of colors is RGB.

- In HSV, hue is a color tone, saturation is the intensity of a color, and value represents its darkness (or brightness at the opposite end of the spectrum).

A quick note on BGR

When I first started dealing with the BGR color space, something wasn't adding up: the [0 255 255] value (no blue, full green, and full red) produces the yellow color. If you have an artistic background, you won't even need to pick up paints and brushes to witness green and red mix into a muddy shade of brown. That is because the color model used in computing is called an **additive** and deals with lights. Lights behave differently from paints (which follow the **subtractive** color model), and—as software runs on computers whose medium is a monitor that emits light—the color model of reference is the additive one.

The Fourier Transform

Much of the processing you apply to images and videos in OpenCV involves the concept of Fourier Transform in some capacity. Joseph Fourier was an 18th century French mathematician who discovered and popularized many mathematical concepts, and concentrated his work on studying the laws governing heat, and in mathematics, all things waveform. In particular, he observed that all waveforms are just the sum of simple sinusoids of different frequencies.

In other words, the waveforms you observe all around you are the sum of other waveforms. This concept is incredibly useful when manipulating images, because it allows us to identify regions in images where a signal (such as image pixels) changes a lot, and regions where the change is less dramatic. We can then arbitrarily mark these regions as noise or regions of interests, background or foreground, and so on. These are the frequencies that make up the original image, and we have the power to separate them to make sense of the image and extrapolate interesting data.

In an OpenCV context, there are a number of algorithms implemented that enable us to process images and make sense of the data contained in them, and these are also reimplemented in NumPy to make our life even easier. NumPy has a **Fast Fourier Transform** (FFT) package, which contains the fft2() method. This method allows us to compute **Discrete Fourier Transform** (DFT) of the image.

Let's examine the **magnitude spectrum** concept of an image using Fourier Transform. The magnitude spectrum of an image is another image, which gives a representation of the original image in terms of its changes: think of it as taking an image and dragging all the brightest pixels to the center. Then, you gradually work your way out to the border where all the darkest pixels have been pushed. Immediately, you will be able to see how many light and dark pixels are contained in your image and the percentage of their distribution.

The concept of Fourier Transform is the basis of many algorithms used for common image processing operations, such as edge detection or line and shape detection.

Before examining these in detail, let's take a look at two concepts that—in conjunction with the Fourier Transform—form the foundation of the aforementioned processing operations: high pass filters and low pass filters.

High pass filter

A **high pass filter** (HPF) is a filter that examines a region of an image and boosts the intensity of certain pixels based on the difference in the intensity with the surrounding pixels.

Take, for example, the following kernel:

```
[[0, -0.25, 0],
 [-0.25, 1, -0.25],
 [0, -0.25, 0]]
```

 A **kernel** is a set of weights that are applied to a region in a source image to generate a single pixel in the destination image. For example, a ksize of 7 implies that 49 (7 x 7) source pixels are considered in generating each destination pixel. We can think of a kernel as a piece of frosted glass moving over the source image and letting through a diffused blend of the source's light.

After calculating the sum of differences of the intensities of the central pixel compared to all the immediate neighbors, the intensity of the central pixel will be boosted (or not) if a high level of changes are found. In other words, if a pixel stands out from the surrounding pixels, it will get boosted.

This is particularly effective in edge detection, where a common form of HPF called high boost filter is used.

Both high pass and low pass filters use a property called radius, which extends the area of the neighbors involved in the filter calculation.

Let's go through an example of an HPF:

```
import cv2
import numpy as np
from scipy import ndimage

kernel_3x3 = np.array([[-1, -1, -1],
                       [-1,  8, -1],
```

```
                        [-1,  -1,  -1]])

kernel_5x5 = np.array([[-1,  -1,  -1,  -1,  -1],
                        [-1,   1,   2,   1,  -1],
                        [-1,   2,   4,   2,  -1],
                        [-1,   1,   2,   1,  -1],
                        [-1,  -1,  -1,  -1,  -1]])
```

 Note that both filters sum up to 0, the reason for this is explained in detail in the *Edge detection* section.

```
img = cv2.imread("../images/color1_small.jpg", 0)

k3 = ndimage.convolve(img, kernel_3x3)
k5 = ndimage.convolve(img, kernel_5x5)

blurred = cv2.GaussianBlur(img, (11,11), 0)
g_hpf = img - blurred

cv2.imshow("3x3", k3)
cv2.imshow("5x5", k5)
cv2.imshow("g_hpf", g_hpf)
cv2.waitKey()
cv2.destroyAllWindows()
```

After the initial imports, we define a 3x3 kernel and a 5x5 kernel, and then we load the image in grayscale. Normally, the majority of image processing is done with NumPy; however, in this particular case, we want to "convolve" an image with a given kernel and NumPy happens to only accept one-dimensional arrays.

This does not mean that the convolution of deep arrays can't be achieved with NumPy, just that it would be a bit complex. Instead, ndimage (which is a part of SciPy, so you should have it installed as per the instructions in *Chapter 1, Setting Up OpenCV*), makes this trivial, through its convolve() function, which supports the classic NumPy arrays that the cv2 modules use to store images.

We apply two HPFs with the two convolution kernels we defined. Lastly, we also implement a differential method of obtaining a HPF by applying a low pass filter and calculating the difference with the original image. You will notice that the third method actually yields the best result, so let's also elaborate on low pass filters.

Low pass filter

If an HPF boosts the intensity of a pixel, given its difference with its neighbors, a **low pass filter (LPF)** will smoothen the pixel if the difference with the surrounding pixels is lower than a certain threshold. This is used in denoising and blurring. For example, one of the most popular blurring/smoothening filters, the Gaussian blur, is a low pass filter that attenuates the intensity of high frequency signals.

Creating modules

As in the case of our `CaptureManager` and `WindowManager` classes, our filters should be reusable outside Cameo. Thus, we should separate the filters into their own Python module or file.

Let's create a file called `filters.py` in the same directory as `cameo.py`. We need the following `import` statements in `filters.py`:

```
import cv2
import numpy
import utils
```

Let's also create a file called `utils.py` in the same directory. It should contain the following `import` statements:

```
import cv2
import numpy
import scipy.interpolate
```

We will be adding filter functions and classes to `filters.py`, while more general-purpose math functions will go in `utils.py`.

Edge detection

Edges play a major role in both human and computer vision. We, as humans, can easily recognize many object types and their pose just by seeing a backlit silhouette or a rough sketch. Indeed, when art emphasizes edges and poses, it often seems to convey the idea of an archetype, such as Rodin's *The Thinker* or Joe Shuster's *Superman*. Software, too, can reason about edges, poses, and archetypes. We will discuss these kinds of reasonings in later chapters.

OpenCV provides many edge-finding filters, including `Laplacian()`, `Sobel()`, and `Scharr()`. These filters are supposed to turn non-edge regions to black while turning edge regions to white or saturated colors. However, they are prone to misidentifying noise as edges. This flaw can be mitigated by blurring an image before trying to find its edges. OpenCV also provides many blurring filters, including `blur()` (simple average), `medianBlur()`, and `GaussianBlur()`. The arguments for the edge-finding and blurring filters vary but always include `ksize`, an odd whole number that represents the width and height (in pixels) of a filter's kernel.

For blurring, let's use `medianBlur()`, which is effective in removing digital video noise, especially in color images. For edge-finding, let's use `Laplacian()`, which produces bold edge lines, especially in grayscale images. After applying `medianBlur()`, but before applying `Laplacian()`, we should convert the image from BGR to grayscale.

Once we have the result of `Laplacian()`, we can invert it to get black edges on a white background. Then, we can normalize it (so that its values range from 0 to 1) and multiply it with the source image to darken the edges. Let's implement this approach in `filters.py`:

```
def strokeEdges(src, dst, blurKsize = 7, edgeKsize = 5):
    if blurKsize >= 3:
        blurredSrc = cv2.medianBlur(src, blurKsize)
        graySrc = cv2.cvtColor(blurredSrc, cv2.COLOR_BGR2GRAY)
    else:
        graySrc = cv2.cvtColor(src, cv2.COLOR_BGR2GRAY)
    cv2.Laplacian(graySrc, cv2.CV_8U, graySrc, ksize = edgeKsize)
    normalizedInverseAlpha = (1.0 / 255) * (255 - graySrc)
    channels = cv2.split(src)
    for channel in channels:
        channel[:] = channel * normalizedInverseAlpha
    cv2.merge(channels, dst)
```

Note that we allow kernel sizes to be specified as arguments for `strokeEdges()`. The `blurKsize` argument is used as `ksize` for `medianBlur()`, while `edgeKsize` is used as `ksize` for `Laplacian()`. With my webcams, I find that a `blurKsize` value of 7 and an `edgeKsize` value of 5 looks best. Unfortunately, `medianBlur()` is expensive with a large `ksize`, such as 7.

 If you encounter performance problems when running `strokeEdges()`, try decreasing the `blurKsize` value. To turn off blur, set it to a value less than 3.

Custom kernels – getting convoluted

As we have just seen, many of OpenCV's predefined filters use a kernel. Remember that a kernel is a set of weights, which determine how each output pixel is calculated from a neighborhood of input pixels. Another term for a kernel is a **convolution matrix**. It mixes up or convolves the pixels in a region. Similarly, a kernel-based filter may be called a convolution filter.

OpenCV provides a very versatile `filter2D()` function, which applies any kernel or convolution matrix that we specify. To understand how to use this function, let's first learn the format of a convolution matrix. It is a 2D array with an odd number of rows and columns. The central element corresponds to a pixel of interest and the other elements correspond to the neighbors of this pixel. Each element contains an integer or floating point value, which is a weight that gets applied to an input pixel's value. Consider this example:

```
kernel = numpy.array([[-1, -1, -1],
                      [-1,  9, -1],
                      [-1, -1, -1]])
```

Here, the pixel of interest has a weight of 9 and its immediate neighbors each have a weight of -1. For the pixel of interest, the output color will be nine times its input color minus the input colors of all eight adjacent pixels. If the pixel of interest is already a bit different from its neighbors, this difference becomes intensified. The effect is that the image looks *sharper* as the contrast between the neighbors is increased.

Continuing our example, we can apply this convolution matrix to a source and destination image, respectively, as follows:

```
cv2.filter2D(src, -1, kernel, dst)
```

The second argument specifies the per-channel depth of the destination image (such as `cv2.CV_8U` for 8 bits per channel). A negative value (as used here) means that the destination image has the same depth as the source image.

For color images, note that `filter2D()` applies the kernel equally to each channel. To use different kernels on different channels, we would also have to use the `split()` and `merge()` functions.

Based on this simple example, let's add two classes to `filters.py`. One class, VConvolutionFilter, will represent a convolution filter in general. A subclass, SharpenFilter, will represent our sharpening filter specifically. Let's edit `filters.py` to implement these two new classes as follows:

```
class VConvolutionFilter(object):
    """A filter that applies a convolution to V (or all of
        BGR)."""

    def __init__(self, kernel):
        self._kernel = kernel

    def apply(self, src, dst):
        """Apply the filter with a BGR or gray source/destination."""
        cv2.filter2D(src, -1, self._kernel, dst)

class SharpenFilter(VConvolutionFilter):
    """A sharpen filter with a 1-pixel radius."""

    def __init__(self):
        kernel = numpy.array([[-1, -1, -1],
                              [-1,  9, -1],
                              [-1, -1, -1]])
        VConvolutionFilter.__init__(self, kernel)
```

Note that the weights sum up to 1. This should be the case whenever we want to leave the image's overall brightness unchanged. If we modify a sharpening kernel slightly so that its weights sum up to 0 instead, we have an edge detection kernel that turns edges white and non-edges black. For example, let's add the following edge detection filter to `filters.py`:

```
class FindEdgesFilter(VConvolutionFilter):
    """An edge-finding filter with a 1-pixel radius."""

    def __init__(self):
        kernel = numpy.array([[-1, -1, -1],
                              [-1,  8, -1],
                              [-1, -1, -1]])
        VConvolutionFilter.__init__(self, kernel)
```

Next, let's make a blur filter. Generally, for a blur effect, the weights should sum up to 1 and should be positive throughout the neighborhood. For example, we can take a simple average of the neighborhood as follows:

```
class BlurFilter(VConvolutionFilter):
    """A blur filter with a 2-pixel radius."""

    def __init__(self):
```

```
kernel = numpy.array([[0.04, 0.04, 0.04, 0.04, 0.04],
                      [0.04, 0.04, 0.04, 0.04, 0.04],
                      [0.04, 0.04, 0.04, 0.04, 0.04],
                      [0.04, 0.04, 0.04, 0.04, 0.04],
                      [0.04, 0.04, 0.04, 0.04, 0.04]])
VConvolutionFilter.__init__(self, kernel)
```

Our sharpening, edge detection, and blur filters use kernels that are highly symmetric. Sometimes, though, kernels with less symmetry produce an interesting effect. Let's consider a kernel that blurs on one side (with positive weights) and sharpens on the other (with negative weights). It will produce a ridged or *embossed* effect. Here is an implementation that we can add to `filters.py`:

```
class EmbossFilter(VConvolutionFilter):
    """An emboss filter with a 1-pixel radius."""

    def __init__(self):
        kernel = numpy.array([[-2, -1, 0],
                              [-1,  1, 1],
                              [ 0,  1, 2]])
        VConvolutionFilter.__init__(self, kernel)
```

This set of custom convolution filters is very basic. Indeed, it is more basic than OpenCV's ready-made set of filters. However, with a bit of experimentation, you should be able to write your own kernels that produce a unique look.

Modifying the application

Now that we have high-level functions and classes for several filters, it is trivial to apply any of them to the captured frames in Cameo. Let's edit `cameo.py` and add the lines that appear in bold face in the following excerpt:

```
import cv2
import filters
from managers import WindowManager, CaptureManager

class Cameo(object):

    def __init__(self):
        self._windowManager = WindowManager('Cameo',
                                             self.onKeypress)
        self._captureManager = CaptureManager(
            cv2.VideoCapture(0), self._windowManager, True)
```

```
        self._curveFilter = filters.BGRPortraCurveFilter()

    def run(self):
        """Run the main loop."""
        self._windowManager.createWindow()
        while self._windowManager.isWindowCreated:
            self._captureManager.enterFrame()
            frame = self._captureManager.frame



            filters.strokeEdges(frame, frame)
            self._curveFilter.apply(frame, frame)

            self._captureManager.exitFrame()
            self._windowManager.processEvents()

    # ... The rest is the same as in Chapter 2.
```

Here, I have chosen to apply two effects: stroking the edges and emulating Portra film colors. Feel free to modify the code to apply any filters you like.

Here is a screenshot from Cameo with stroked edges and Portra-like colors:

Edge detection with Canny

OpenCV also offers a very handy function called Canny (after the algorithm's inventor, John F. Canny), which is very popular not only because of its effectiveness, but also the simplicity of its implementation in an OpenCV program, as it is a one-liner:

```
import cv2
import numpy as np

img = cv2.imread("../images/statue_small.jpg", 0)
cv2.imwrite("canny.jpg", cv2.Canny(img, 200, 300))
cv2.imshow("canny", cv2.imread("canny.jpg"))
cv2.waitKey()
cv2.destroyAllWindows()
```

The result is a very clear identification of the edges:

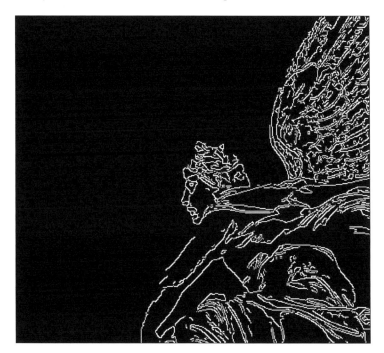

The Canny edge detection algorithm is quite complex but also interesting: it's a five-step process that denoises the image with a Gaussian filter, calculates gradients, applies **non maximum suppression (NMS)** on edges, a double threshold on all the detected edges to eliminate false positives, and, lastly, analyzes all the edges and their connection to each other to keep the real edges and discard the weak ones.

Contour detection

Another vital task in computer vision is contour detection, not only because of the obvious aspect of detecting contours of subjects contained in an image or video frame, but because of the derivative operations connected with identifying contours.

These operations are, namely, computing bounding polygons, approximating shapes, and generally calculating regions of interest, which considerably simplify interaction with image data because a rectangular region with NumPy is easily defined with an array slice. We will be using this technique a lot when exploring the concept of object detection (including faces) and object tracking.

Let's go in order and familiarize ourselves with the API first with an example:

```
import cv2
import numpy as np

img = np.zeros((200, 200), dtype=np.uint8)
img[50:150, 50:150] = 255

ret, thresh = cv2.threshold(img, 127, 255, 0)
image, contours, hierarchy = cv2.findContours(thresh,
    cv2.RETR_TREE, cv2.CHAIN_APPROX_SIMPLE)
color = cv2.cvtColor(img, cv2.COLOR_GRAY2BGR)
img = cv2.drawContours(color, contours, -1, (0,255,0), 2)
cv2.imshow("contours", color)
cv2.waitKey()
cv2.destroyAllWindows()
```

Firstly, we create an empty black image that is 200x200 pixels in size. Then, we place a white square in the center of it utilizing ndarray's ability to assign values on a slice.

We then threshold the image, and call the `findContours()` function. This function has three parameters: the input image, hierarchy type, and the contour approximation method. There are a number of aspects that are of particular interest in this function:

- The function modifies the input image, so it would be advisable to use a copy of the original image (for example, by passing `img.copy()`).

- Secondly, the hierarchy tree returned by the function is quite important: `cv2.RETR_TREE` will retrieve the entire hierarchy of contours in the image, enabling you to establish "relationships" between contours. If you only want to retrieve the most external contours, use `cv2.RETR_EXTERNAL`. This is particularly useful when you want to eliminate contours that are entirely contained in other contours (for example, in a vast majority of cases, you won't need to detect an object within another object of the same type).

The `findContours` function returns three elements: the modified image, contours, and their hierarchy. We use the contours to draw on the color version of the image (so that we can draw contours in green) and eventually display it.

The result is a white square with its contour drawn in green. Spartan, but effective in demonstrating the concept! Let's move on to more meaningful examples.

Contours – bounding box, minimum area rectangle, and minimum enclosing circle

Finding the contours of a square is a simple task; irregular, skewed, and rotated shapes bring the best out of the `cv2.findContours` utility function of OpenCV. Let's take a look at the following image:

In a real-life application, we would be most interested in determining the bounding box of the subject, its minimum enclosing rectangle, and its circle. The `cv2.findContours` function in conjunction with a few other OpenCV utilities makes this very easy to accomplish:

```
import cv2
import numpy as np

img = cv2.pyrDown(cv2.imread("hammer.jpg", cv2.IMREAD_UNCHANGED))

ret, thresh = cv2.threshold(cv2.cvtColor(img.copy(),
    cv2.COLOR_BGR2GRAY) , 127, 255, cv2.THRESH_BINARY)
```

```
    image, contours, hier = cv2.findContours(thresh,
        cv2.RETR_EXTERNAL, cv2.CHAIN_APPROX_SIMPLE)

    for c in contours:
      # find bounding box coordinates
      x,y,w,h = cv2.boundingRect(c)
      cv2.rectangle(img, (x,y), (x+w, y+h), (0, 255, 0), 2)

      # find minimum area
      rect = cv2.minAreaRect(c)
      # calculate coordinates of the minimum area rectangle
      box = cv2.boxPoints(rect)
      # normalize coordinates to integers
      box = np.int0(box)
      # draw contours
      cv2.drawContours(img, [box], 0, (0,0, 255), 3)

      # calculate center and radius of minimum enclosing circle
      (x,y),radius = cv2.minEnclosingCircle(c)
      # cast to integers
      center = (int(x),int(y))
      radius = int(radius)
      # draw the circle
      img = cv2.circle(img,center,radius,(0,255,0),2)

    cv2.drawContours(img, contours, -1, (255, 0, 0), 1)
    cv2.imshow("contours", img)
```

After the initial imports, we load the image, and then apply a binary threshold on a grayscale version of the original image. By doing this, we operate all find-contour calculations on a grayscale copy, but we draw on the original so that we can utilize color information.

Firstly, let's calculate a simple bounding box:

```
    x,y,w,h = cv2.boundingRect(c)
```

This is a pretty straightforward conversion of contour information to the (x, y) coordinates, plus the height and width of the rectangle. Drawing this rectangle is an easy task and can be done using this code:

```
    cv2.rectangle(img, (x,y), (x+w, y+h), (0, 255, 0), 2)
```

Secondly, let's calculate the minimum area enclosing the subject:

```
rect = cv2.minAreaRect(c)
box = cv2.boxPoints(rect)
  box = np.int0(box)
```

The mechanism used here is particularly interesting: OpenCV does not have a function to calculate the coordinates of the minimum rectangle vertexes directly from the contour information. Instead, we calculate the minimum rectangle area, and then calculate the vertexes of this rectangle. Note that the calculated vertexes are floats, but pixels are accessed with integers (you can't access a "portion" of a pixel), so we need to operate this conversion. Next, we draw the box, which gives us the perfect opportunity to introduce the `cv2.drawContours` function:

```
cv2.drawContours(img, [box], 0, (0,0, 255), 3)
```

Firstly, this function—like all drawing functions—modifies the original image. Secondly, it takes an array of contours in its second parameter, so you can draw a number of contours in a single operation. Therefore, if you have a single set of points representing a contour polygon, you need to wrap these points into an array, exactly like we did with our box in the preceding example. The third parameter of this function specifies the index of the contours array that we want to draw: a value of `-1` will draw all contours; otherwise, a contour at the specified index in the contours array (the second parameter) will be drawn.

Most drawing functions take the color of the drawing and its thickness as the last two parameters.

The last bounding contour we're going to examine is the minimum enclosing circle:

```
(x,y),radius = cv2.minEnclosingCircle(c)
center = (int(x),int(y))
radius = int(radius)
img = cv2.circle(img,center,radius,(0,255,0),2)
```

The only peculiarity of the `cv2.minEnclosingCircle` function is that it returns a two-element tuple, of which the first element is a tuple itself, representing the coordinates of the circle's center, and the second element is the radius of this circle. After converting all these values to integers, drawing the circle is quite a trivial operation.

The final result on the original image looks like this:

Contours – convex contours and the Douglas-Peucker algorithm

Most of the time, when working with contours, subjects will have the most diverse shapes, including convex ones. A convex shape is one where there are two points within this shape whose connecting line goes outside the perimeter of the shape itself.

The first facility that OpenCV offers to calculate the approximate bounding polygon of a shape is cv2.approxPolyDP. This function takes three parameters:

- A contour
- An epsilon value representing the maximum discrepancy between the original contour and the approximated polygon (the lower the value, the closer the approximated value will be to the original contour)
- A Boolean flag signifying that the polygon is closed

The epsilon value is of vital importance to obtain a useful contour, so let's understand what it represents. An epsilon is the maximum difference between the approximated polygon's perimeter and the original contour's perimeter. The lower this difference is, the more the approximated polygon will be similar to the original contour.

You may ask yourself why we need an approximate polygon when we have a contour that is already a precise representation. The answer to this is that a polygon is a set of straight lines, and the importance of being able to define polygons in a region for further manipulation and processing is paramount in many computer vision tasks.

Now that we know what an epsilon is, we need to obtain contour perimeter information as a reference value. This is obtained with the `cv2.arcLength` function of OpenCV:

```
epsilon = 0.01 * cv2.arcLength(cnt, True)
approx = cv2.approxPolyDP(cnt, epsilon, True)
```

Effectively, we're instructing OpenCV to calculate an approximated polygon whose perimeter can only differ from the original contour in an epsilon ratio.

OpenCV also offers a `cv2.convexHull` function to obtain processed contour information for convex shapes and this is a straightforward one-line expression:

```
hull = cv2.convexHull(cnt)
```

Let's combine the original contour, approximated polygon contour, and the convex hull in one image to observe the difference between them. To simplify things, I've applied the contours to a black image so that the original subject is not visible but its contours are:

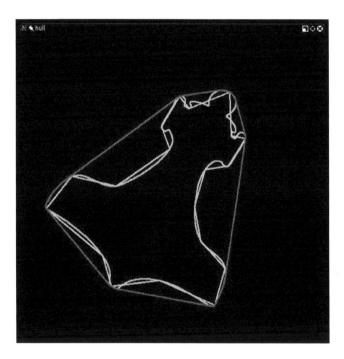

As you can see, the convex hull surrounds the entire subject, the approximated polygon is the innermost polygon shape, and in between the two is the original contour, mainly composed of arcs.

Line and circle detection

Detecting edges and contours are not only common and important tasks, they also constitute the basis for other complex operations. Lines and shape detection go hand in hand with edge and contour detection, so let's examine how OpenCV implements these.

The theory behind lines and shape detection has its foundation in a technique called the Hough transform, invented by Richard Duda and Peter Hart, who extended (generalized) the work done by Paul Hough in the early 1960s.

Let's take a look at OpenCV's API for the Hough transforms.

Line detection

First of all, let's detect some lines, which is done with the HoughLines and HoughLinesP functions. The only difference between the two functions is that one uses the standard Hough transform, and the second uses the probabilistic Hough transform (hence P in the name).

The probabilistic version is so-called because it only analyzes a subset of points and estimates the probability of these points all belonging to the same line. This implementation is an optimized version of the standard Hough transform, and in this case, it's less computationally intensive and executes faster.

Let's take a look at a very simple example:

```python
import cv2
import numpy as np

img = cv2.imread('lines.jpg')
gray = cv2.cvtColor(img,cv2.COLOR_BGR2GRAY)
edges = cv2.Canny(gray,50,120)
minLineLength = 20
maxLineGap = 5
lines =
    cv2.HoughLinesP(edges,1,np.pi/180,100,minLineLength,
        maxLineGap)
for x1,y1,x2,y2 in lines[0]:
  cv2.line(img,(x1,y1),(x2,y2),(0,255,0),2)

cv2.imshow("edges", edges)
cv2.imshow("lines", img)
cv2.waitKey()
cv2.destroyAllWindows()
```

The crucial point of this simple script—aside from the `HoughLines` function call—is the setting of minimum line length (shorter lines will be discarded) and the maximum line gap, which is the maximum size of a gap in a line before the two segments start being considered as separate lines.

Also note that the `HoughLines` function takes a single channel binary image, processed through the Canny edge detection filter. Canny is not a strict requirement, however; an image that's been denoised and only represents edges, is the ideal source for a Hough transform, so you will find this to be a common practice.

The parameters of `HoughLinesP` are as follows:

- The image we want to process.

- The geometrical representations of the lines, `rho` and `theta`, which are usually `1` and `np.pi/180`.

- The threshold, which represents the threshold below which a line is discarded. The Hough transform works with a system of bins and votes, with each bin representing a line, so any line with a minimum of the `<threshold>` votes is retained, the rest discarded.

- `MinLineLength` and `MaxLineGap`, which we mentioned previously.

Circle detection

OpenCV also has a function for detecting circles, called `HoughCircles`. It works in a very similar fashion to `HoughLines`, but where `minLineLength` and `maxLineGap` were the parameters to discard or retain lines, `HoughCircles` has a minimum distance between circles' centers, minimum, and maximum radius of the circles. Here's the obligatory example:

```
import cv2
import numpy as np

planets = cv2.imread('planet_glow.jpg')
gray_img = cv2.cvtColor(planets, cv2.COLOR_BGR2GRAY)
img = cv2.medianBlur(gray_img, 5)
cimg = cv2.cvtColor(img,cv2.COLOR_GRAY2BGR)

circles = cv2.HoughCircles(img,cv2.HOUGH_GRADIENT,1,120,
                            param1=100,param2=30,minRadius=0,
                                maxRadius=0)

circles = np.uint16(np.around(circles))

for i in circles[0,:]:
```

```
# draw the outer circle
cv2.circle(planets,(i[0],i[1]),i[2],(0,255,0),2)
# draw the center of the circle
cv2.circle(planets,(i[0],i[1]),2,(0,0,255),3)

cv2.imwrite("planets_circles.jpg", planets)
cv2.imshow("HoughCirlces", planets)
cv2.waitKey()
cv2.destroyAllWindows()
```

Here's a visual representation of the result:

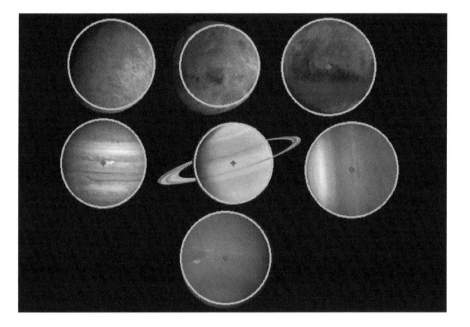

Detecting shapes

The detection of shapes with the Hough transform is limited to circles; however, we already implicitly explored detecting shapes of any kind, specifically when we talked about approxPolyDP. This function allows the approximation of polygons, so if your image contains polygons, they will be quite accurately detected, combining the usage of cv2.findContours and cv2.approxPolyDP.

Summary

At this point, you should have gained a good understanding of color spaces, Fourier Transform, and the several kinds of filters made available by OpenCV to process images.

You should also be proficient in detecting edges, lines, circles, and shapes in general. Additionally, you should be able to find contours and exploit the information they provide about the subjects contained in an image. These concepts will serve as the ideal background to explore the topics in the next chapter.

4
Depth Estimation and Segmentation

This chapter shows you how to use data from a depth camera to identify foreground and background regions, so that we can limit an effect to only the foreground or only the background. As prerequisites, we need a depth camera, such as Microsoft Kinect, and we need to build OpenCV with support for our depth camera. For build instructions, see *Chapter 1*, *Setting Up OpenCV*.

We'll deal with two main topics in this chapter: depth estimation and segmentation. We will explore depth estimation with two distinct approaches: firstly, by using a depth camera (a prerequisite of the first part of the chapter), such as Microsoft Kinect, and then, by using stereo images, for which a normal camera will suffice. For instructions on how to build OpenCV with support for depth cameras, see *Chapter 1*, *Setting Up OpenCV*. The second part of the chapter is about segmentation, the technique that allows us to extract foreground objects from an image.

Creating modules

The code to capture and manipulate depth-camera data will be reusable outside `Cameo.py`. So, we should separate it into a new module. Let's create a file called `depth.py` in the same directory as `Cameo.py`. We need the following `import` statement in `depth.py`:

```
import numpy
```

We will also need to modify our preexisting `rects.py` file so that our copy operations can be limited to a nonrectangular subregion of a rectangle. To support the changes we are going to make, let's add the following `import` statements to `rects.py`:

```
import numpy
import utils
```

Finally, the new version of our application will use depth-related functionalities. So, let's add the following `import` statement to `Cameo.py`:

```
import depth
```

Now, let's go deeper into the subject of depth.

Capturing frames from a depth camera

Back in *Chapter 2, Handling Files, Cameras, and GUIs*, we discussed the concept that a computer can have multiple video capture devices and each device can have multiple channels. Suppose a given device is a stereo camera. Each channel might correspond to a different lens and sensor. Also, each channel might correspond to different kinds of data, such as a normal color image versus a depth map. The C++ version of OpenCV defines some constants for the identifiers of certain devices and channels. However, these constants are not defined in the Python version.

To remedy this situation, let's add the following definitions in `depth.py`:

```
# Devices.CAP_OPENNI = 900 # OpenNI (for Microsoft
    Kinect)CAP_OPENNI_ASUS = 910 # OpenNI (for Asus Xtion)
# Channels of an OpenNI-compatible depth
    generator.CAP_OPENNI_DEPTH_MAP = 0 # Depth values in mm
        (16UC1)CAP_OPENNI_POINT_CLOUD_MAP = 1 # XYZ in meters
            (32FC3)CAP_OPENNI_DISPARITY_MAP = 2 # Disparity in
                pixels (8UC1)CAP_OPENNI_DISPARITY_MAP_32F = 3 #
                    Disparity in pixels
                        (32FC1)CAP_OPENNI_VALID_DEPTH_MASK = 4 #
                            8UC1
# Channels of an OpenNI-compatible RGB image
    generator.CAP_OPENNI_BGR_IMAGE = 5CAP_OPENNI_GRAY_IMAGE = 6
```

The depth-related channels require some explanation, as given in the following list:

- A **depth map** is a grayscale image in which each pixel value is the estimated distance from the camera to a surface. Specifically, an image from the `CAP_OPENNI_DEPTH_MAP` channel gives the distance as a floating-point number of millimeters.

- A **point cloud map** is a color image in which each color corresponds to an (x, y, or z) spatial dimension. Specifically, the `CAP_OPENNI_POINT_CLOUD_MAP` channel yields a BGR image, where B is x (blue is right), G is y (green is up), and R is z (red is deep), from the camera's perspective. The values are in meters.

- A **disparity map** is a grayscale image in which each pixel value is the stereo disparity of a surface. To conceptualize stereo disparity, let's suppose we overlay two images of a scene, shot from different viewpoints. The result would be similar to seeing double images. For points on any pair of twin objects in the scene, we can measure the distance in pixels. This measurement is the stereo disparity. Nearby objects exhibit greater stereo disparity than far-off objects. Thus, nearby objects appear brighter in a disparity map.

- A **valid depth mask** shows whether the depth information at a given pixel is believed to be valid (shown by a nonzero value) or invalid (shown by a value of zero). For example, if the depth camera depends on an infrared illuminator (an infrared flash), depth information is invalid in regions that are occluded (shadowed) from this light.

The following screenshot shows a point cloud map of a man sitting behind a sculpture of a cat:

The following screenshot has a disparity map of a man sitting behind a sculpture of a cat:

A valid depth mask of a man sitting behind a sculpture of a cat is shown in the following screenshot:

Creating a mask from a disparity map

For the purposes of Cameo, we are interested in disparity maps and valid depth masks. They can help us refine our estimates of facial regions.

Using the `FaceTracker` function and a normal color image, we can obtain rectangular estimates of facial regions. By analyzing such a rectangular region in the corresponding disparity map, we can tell that some pixels within the rectangle are outliers—too near or too far to really be a part of the face. We can refine the facial region to exclude these outliers. However, we should only apply this test where the data is valid, as indicated by the valid depth mask.

Let's write a function to generate a mask whose values are 0 for the rejected regions of the facial rectangle and 1 for the accepted regions. This function should take a disparity map, valid depth mask, and a rectangle as arguments. We can implement it in `depth.py` as follows:

```
def createMedianMask(disparityMap, validDepthMask, rect = None):
    """Return a mask selecting the median layer, plus shadows."""
    if rect is not None:
        x, y, w, h = rect
        disparityMap = disparityMap[y:y+h, x:x+w]
        validDepthMask = validDepthMask[y:y+h, x:x+w]
    median = numpy.median(disparityMap)
    return numpy.where((validDepthMask == 0) | \
                          (abs(disparityMap - median) < 12),
                       1.0, 0.0)
```

To identify outliers in the disparity map, we first find the median using `numpy.median()`, which takes an array as an argument. If the array is of an odd length, `median()` returns the value that would lie in the middle of the array if the array were sorted. If the array is of even length, `median()` returns the average of the two values that would be sorted nearest to the middle of the array.

To generate a mask based on per-pixel Boolean operations, we use `numpy.where()` with three arguments. In the first argument, `where()` takes an array whose elements are evaluated for truth or falsity. An output array of like dimensions is returned. Wherever an element in the input array is `true`, the `where()` function's second argument is assigned to the corresponding element in the output array. Conversely, wherever an element in the input array is `false`, the `where()` function's third argument is assigned to the corresponding element in the output array.

Our implementation treats a pixel as an outlier when it has a valid disparity value that deviates from the median disparity value by 12 or more. I've chosen the value of 12 just by experimentation. Feel free to tweak this value later based on the results you encounter when running Cameo with your particular camera setup.

Masking a copy operation

As part of the previous chapter's work, we wrote copyRect() as a copy operation that limits itself to the given rectangles of a source and destination image. Now, we want to apply further limits to this copy operation. We want to use a given mask that has the same dimensions as the source rectangle.

We shall copy only those pixels in the source rectangle where the mask's value is not zero. Other pixels shall retain their old values from the destination image. This logic, with an array of conditions and two arrays of possible output values, can be expressed concisely with the numpy.where() function that we have recently learned.

Let's open rects.py and edit copyRect() to add a new mask argument. This argument may be None, in which case, we fall back to our old implementation of the copy operation. Otherwise, we next ensure that mask and the images have the same number of channels. We assume that mask has one channel but the images may have three channels (BGR). We can add duplicate channels to mask using the repeat() and reshape() methods of numpy.array.

Finally, we perform the copy operation using where(). The complete implementation is as follows:

```
def copyRect(src, dst, srcRect, dstRect, mask = None,
             interpolation = cv2.INTER_LINEAR):
    """Copy part of the source to part of the destination."""

    x0, y0, w0, h0 = srcRect
    x1, y1, w1, h1 = dstRect

    # Resize the contents of the source sub-rectangle.
    # Put the result in the destination sub-rectangle.
    if mask is None:
        dst[y1:y1+h1, x1:x1+w1] = \
            cv2.resize(src[y0:y0+h0, x0:x0+w0], (w1, h1),
                       interpolation = interpolation)
    else:
        if not utils.isGray(src):
            # Convert the mask to 3 channels, like the image.
```

```
        mask = mask.repeat(3).reshape(h0, w0, 3)
    # Perform the copy, with the mask applied.
    dst[y1:y1+h1, x1:x1+w1] = \
        numpy.where(cv2.resize(mask, (w1, h1),
                               interpolation = \
                               cv2.INTER_NEAREST),
                cv2.resize(src[y0:y0+h0, x0:x0+w0], (w1,
                    h1),
                               interpolation = interpolation),
                dst[y1:y1+h1, x1:x1+w1])
```

We also need to modify our swapRects() function, which uses copyRect() to perform a circular swap of a list of rectangular regions. The modifications to swapRects() are quite simple. We just need to add a new masks argument, which is a list of masks whose elements are passed to the respective copyRect() calls. If the value of the given masks argument is None, we pass None to every copyRect() call.

The following code shows you the full implementation of this:

```
def swapRects(src, dst, rects, masks = None,
              interpolation = cv2.INTER_LINEAR):
    """Copy the source with two or more sub-rectangles swapped."""

    if dst is not src:
        dst[:] = src

    numRects = len(rects)
    if numRects < 2:
        return

    if masks is None:
        masks = [None] * numRects

    # Copy the contents of the last rectangle into temporary
        storage.
    x, y, w, h = rects[numRects - 1]
    temp = src[y:y+h, x:x+w].copy()

    # Copy the contents of each rectangle into the next.
    i = numRects - 2
    while i >= 0:
        copyRect(src, dst, rects[i], rects[i+1], masks[i],
```

```
                    interpolation)
        i -= 1

    # Copy the temporarily stored content into the first rectangle.
    copyRect(temp, dst, (0, 0, w, h), rects[0], masks[numRects -
        1],
            interpolation)
```

Note that the `masks` argument in `copyRect()` and `swapRects()` both default to `None`. Thus, our new versions of these functions are backward compatible with our previous versions of Cameo.

Depth estimation with a normal camera

A depth camera is a fantastic little device to capture images and estimate the distance of objects from the camera itself, but, how does the depth camera retrieve depth information? Also, is it possible to reproduce the same kind of calculations with a normal camera?

A depth camera, such as Microsoft Kinect, uses a traditional camera combined with an infrared sensor that helps the camera differentiate similar objects and calculate their distance from the camera. However, not everybody has access to a depth camera or a Kinect, and especially when you're just learning OpenCV, you're probably not going to invest in an expensive piece of equipment until you feel your skills are well-sharpened, and your interest in the subject is confirmed.

Our setup includes a simple camera, which is most likely integrated in our machine, or a webcam attached to our computer. So, we need to resort to less fancy means of estimating the difference in distance of objects from the camera.

Geometry will come to the rescue in this case, and in particular, Epipolar Geometry, which is the geometry of stereo vision. Stereo vision is a branch of computer vision that extracts three-dimensional information out of two different images of the same subject.

How does epipolar geometry work? Conceptually, it traces imaginary lines from the camera to each object in the image, then does the same on the second image, and calculates the distance of objects based on the intersection of the lines corresponding to the same object. Here is a representation of this concept:

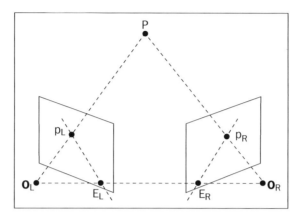

Let's see how OpenCV applies epipolar geometry to calculate a so-called disparity map, which is basically a representation of the different depths detected in the images. This will enable us to extract the foreground of a picture and discard the rest.

Firstly, we need two images of the same subject taken from different points of view, but paying attention to the fact that the pictures are taken at an equal distance from the object, otherwise the calculations will fail and the disparity map will be meaningless.

So, moving on to an example:

```
import numpy as np
import cv2

def update(val = 0):
    # disparity range is tuned for 'aloe' image pair
    stereo.setBlockSize(cv2.getTrackbarPos('window_size',
        'disparity'))
    stereo.setUniquenessRatio(cv2.getTrackbarPos
        ('uniquenessRatio', 'disparity'))
    stereo.setSpeckleWindowSize(cv2.getTrackbarPos
        ('speckleWindowSize', 'disparity'))
    stereo.setSpeckleRange(cv2.getTrackbarPos('speckleRange',
        'disparity'))
    stereo.setDisp12MaxDiff(cv2.getTrackbarPos('disp12MaxDiff',
        'disparity'))

    print 'computing disparity...'
```

```
        disp = stereo.compute(imgL, imgR).astype(np.float32) / 16.0

        cv2.imshow('left', imgL)
        cv2.imshow('disparity', (disp-min_disp)/num_disp)


if __name__ == "__main__":
    window_size = 5
    min_disp = 16
    num_disp = 192-min_disp
    blockSize = window_size
    uniquenessRatio = 1
    speckleRange = 3
    speckleWindowSize = 3
    disp12MaxDiff = 200
    P1 = 600
    P2 = 2400
    imgL = cv2.imread('images/color1_small.jpg')
    imgR = cv2.imread('images/color2_small.jpg')
    cv2.namedWindow('disparity')
    cv2.createTrackbar('speckleRange', 'disparity', speckleRange,
        50, update)
    cv2.createTrackbar('window_size', 'disparity', window_size,
        21, update)
    cv2.createTrackbar('speckleWindowSize', 'disparity',
        speckleWindowSize, 200, update)
    cv2.createTrackbar('uniquenessRatio', 'disparity',
        uniquenessRatio, 50, update)
    cv2.createTrackbar('disp12MaxDiff', 'disparity',
        disp12MaxDiff, 250, update)
    stereo = cv2.StereoSGBM_create(
        minDisparity = min_disp,
        numDisparities = num_disp,
        blockSize = window_size,
        uniquenessRatio = uniquenessRatio,
        speckleRange = speckleRange,
        speckleWindowSize = speckleWindowSize,
        disp12MaxDiff = disp12MaxDiff,
        P1 = P1,
        P2 = P2
    )
    update()
    cv2.waitKey()
```

In this example, we take two images of the same subject and calculate a disparity map, showing in brighter colors the points in the map that are closer to the camera. The areas marked in black represent the disparities.

First of all, we import numpy and cv2 as usual.

Let's skip the definition of the update function for a second and take a look at the main code; the process is quite simple: load two images, create a StereoSGBM instance (StereoSGBM stands for **semiglobal block matching**, and it is an algorithm used for computing disparity maps), and also create a few trackbars to play around with the parameters of the algorithm and call the update function.

The update function applies the trackbar values to the StereoSGBM instance, and then calls the compute method, which produces a disparity map. All in all, pretty simple! Here is the first image I've used:

This is the second one:

There you go: a nice and quite easy to interpret disparity map.

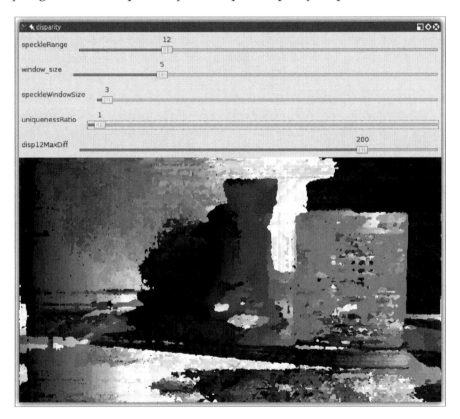

The parameters used by `StereoSGBM` are as follows (taken from the OpenCV documentation):

Parameter	Description
minDisparity	This parameter refers to the minimum possible disparity value. Normally, it is zero but sometimes, rectification algorithms can shift images, so this parameter needs to be adjusted accordingly.
numDisparities	This parameter refers to the maximum disparity minus minimum disparity. The resultant value is always greater than zero. In the current implementation, this parameter must be divisible by 16.
windowSize	This parameter refers to a matched block size. It must be an odd number greater than or equal to 1. Normally, it should be somewhere in the 3-11 range.
P1	This parameter refers to the first parameter controlling the disparity smoothness. See the next point.
P2	This parameter refers to the second parameter that controls the disparity smoothness. The larger the values are, the smoother the disparity is. P1 is the penalty on the disparity change by plus or minus 1 between neighbor pixels. P2 is the penalty on the disparity change by more than 1 between neighbor pixels. The algorithm requires P2 > P1.
	See the `stereo_match.cpp` sample where some reasonably good P1 and P2 values are shown (such as `8*number_of_image_channels*windowSize*windowSize` and `32*number_of_image_channels*windowSize*windowSize`, respectively).
disp12MaxDiff	This parameter refers to the maximum allowed difference (in integer pixel units) in the left-right disparity check. Set it to a nonpositive value to disable the check.
preFilterCap	This parameter refers to the truncation value for prefiltered image pixels. The algorithm first computes the x-derivative at each pixel and clips its value by the `[-preFilterCap, preFilterCap]` interval. The resultant values are passed to the Birchfield-Tomasi pixel cost function.
uniquenessRatio	This parameter refers to the margin in percentage by which the best (minimum) computed cost function value should "win" the second best value to consider the found match to be correct. Normally, a value within the 5-15 range is good enough.

Parameter	Description
speckleWindowSize	This parameter refers to the maximum size of smooth disparity regions to consider their noise speckles and invalidate. Set it to 0 to disable speckle filtering. Otherwise, set it somewhere in the 50-200 range.
speckleRange	This parameter refers to the maximum disparity variation within each connected component. If you do speckle filtering, set the parameter to a positive value; it will implicitly be multiplied by 16. Normally, 1 or 2 is good enough.

With the preceding script, you'll be able to load the images and play around with parameters until you're happy with the disparity map generated by StereoSGBM.

Object segmentation using the Watershed and GrabCut algorithms

Calculating a disparity map can be very useful to detect the foreground of an image, but StereoSGBM is not the only algorithm available to accomplish this, and in fact, StereoSGBM is more about gathering 3D information from 2D pictures, than anything else. **GrabCut**, however, is a perfect tool for this purpose. The GrabCut algorithm follows a precise sequence of steps:

1. A rectangle including the subject(s) of the picture is defined.

2. The area lying outside the rectangle is automatically defined as a background.

3. The data contained in the background is used as a reference to distinguish background areas from foreground areas within the user-defined rectangle.

4. A **Gaussians Mixture Model (GMM)** models the foreground and background, and labels undefined pixels as probable background and foregrounds.

5. Each pixel in the image is virtually connected to the surrounding pixels through virtual edges, and each edge gets a probability of being foreground or background, based on how similar it is in color to the pixels surrounding it.

6. Each pixel (or node as it is conceptualized in the algorithm) is connected to either a foreground or a background node, which you can picture looking like this:

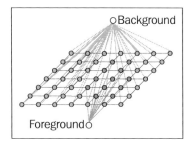

7. After the nodes have been connected to either terminal (background or foreground, also called a source and sink), the edges between nodes belonging to different terminals are cut (the famous cut part of the algorithm), which enables the separation of the parts of the image. This graph adequately represents the algorithm:

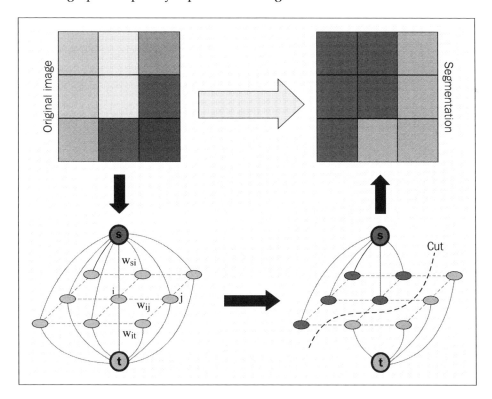

Example of foreground detection with GrabCut

Let's look at an example. We start with the picture of a beautiful statue of an angel.

We want to grab our angel and discard the background. To do this, we will create a relatively short script that will instantiate GrabCut, operate the separation, and then display the resulting image side by side to the original. We will do this using `matplotlib`, a very useful Python library, which makes displaying charts and images a trivial task:

```python
import numpy as np
import cv2
from matplotlib import pyplot as plt

img = cv2.imread('images/statue_small.jpg')
mask = np.zeros(img.shape[:2],np.uint8)

bgdModel = np.zeros((1,65),np.float64)
fgdModel = np.zeros((1,65),np.float64)

rect = (100,50,421,378)
cv2.grabCut(img,mask,rect,bgdModel,fgdModel,5,
    cv2.GC_INIT_WITH_RECT)

mask2 = np.where((mask==2)|(mask==0),0,1).astype('uint8')
```

```
img = img*mask2[:,:,np.newaxis]

plt.subplot(121), plt.imshow(img)
plt.title("grabcut"), plt.xticks([]), plt.yticks([])
plt.subplot(122), plt.imshow(cv2.cvtColor(cv2.imread('images/statue_
small.jpg'),
    cv2.COLOR_BGR2RGB))
plt.title("original"), plt.xticks([]), plt.yticks([])
plt.show()
```

This code is actually quite straightforward. Firstly, we load the image we want to process, and then we create a mask populated with zeros with the same shape as the image we've loaded:

```
import numpy as np
import cv2
from matplotlib import pyplot as plt

img = cv2.imread('images/statue_small.jpg')
mask = np.zeros(img.shape[:2],np.uint8)
```

We then create zero-filled foreground and background models:

```
bgdModel = np.zeros((1,65),np.float64)
fgdModel = np.zeros((1,65),np.float64)
```

We could have populated these models with data, but we're going to initialize the GrabCut algorithm with a rectangle identifying the subject we want to isolate. So, background and foreground models are going to be determined based on the areas left out of the initial rectangle. This rectangle is defined in the next line:

```
rect = (100,50,421,378)
```

Now to the interesting part! We run the GrabCut algorithm specifying the empty models and mask, and the fact that we're going to use a rectangle to initialize the operation:

```
cv2.grabCut(img,mask,rect,bgdModel,fgdModel,5,
    cv2.GC_INIT_WITH_RECT)
```

You'll also notice an integer after `fgdModel`, which is the number of iterations the algorithm is going to run on the image. You can increase these, but there is a point in which pixel classifications will converge, and effectively, you'll just be adding iterations without obtaining any more improvements.

After this, our mask will have changed to contain values between 0 and 3. The values, 0 and 2, will be converted into zeros, and 1-3 into ones, and stored into mask2, which we can then use to filter out all zero-value pixels (theoretically leaving all foreground pixels intact):

```
mask2 = np.where((mask==2)|(mask==0),0,1).astype('uint8')
img = img*mask2[:,:,np.newaxis]
```

The last part of the code displays the images side by side, and here's the result:

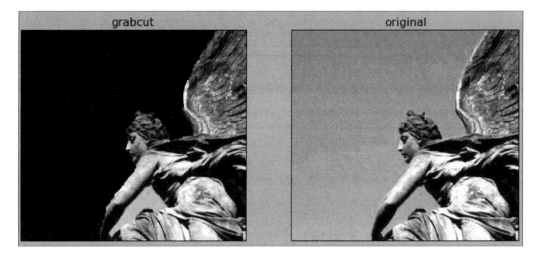

This is quite a satisfactory result. You'll notice that an area of background is left under the angel's arm. It is possible to apply touch strokes to apply more iterations; the technique is quite well illustrated in the grabcut.py file in samples/python2 of your OpenCV installation.

Image segmentation with the Watershed algorithm

Finally, we take a quick look at the Watershed algorithm. The algorithm is called Watershed, because its conceptualization involves water. Imagine areas with low density (little to no change) in an image as valleys, and areas with high density (lots of change) as peaks. Start filling the valleys with water to the point where water from two different valleys is about to merge. To prevent the merging of water from different valleys, you build a barrier to keep them separated. The resulting barrier is the image segmentation.

As an Italian, I love food, and one of the things I love the most is a good plate of pasta with a pesto sauce. So here's a picture of the most vital ingredient for a pesto, basil:

Now, we want to segment the image to separate the basil leaves from the white background.

Once more, we import numpy, cv2, and matplotlib, and then import our basil leaves' image:

```
import numpy as np
import cv2
from matplotlib import pyplot as plt
img = cv2.imread('images/basil.jpg')
gray = cv2.cvtColor(img,cv2.COLOR_BGR2GRAY)
```

After changing the color to grayscale, we run a threshold on the image. This operation helps dividing the image in two, blacks and whites:

```
ret, thresh = cv2.threshold
    (gray,0,255,cv2.THRESH_BINARY_INV+cv2.THRESH_OTSU)
```

Next up, we remove noise from the image by applying the morphologyEx transformation, an operation that consists of dilating and then eroding an image to extract features:

```
kernel = np.ones((3,3),np.uint8)
opening = cv2.morphologyEx(thresh,cv2.MORPH_OPEN,kernel,
    iterations = 2)
```

By dilating the result of the morphology transformation, we can obtain areas of the image that are most certainly background:

```
sure_bg = cv2.dilate(opening,kernel,iterations=3)
```

Conversely, we can obtain sure foreground areas by applying `distanceTransform`. In practical terms, of all the areas most likely to be foreground, the farther away from the "border" with the background a point is, the higher the chance it is foreground. Once we've obtained the `distanceTransform` representation of the image, we apply a threshold to determine with a highly mathematical probability whether the areas are foreground:

```
dist_transform = cv2.distanceTransform(opening,cv2.DIST_L2,5)
ret, sure_fg =
    cv2.threshold(dist_transform,0.7*dist_transform.max(),255,0)
```

At this stage, we have some `sure` foregrounds and backgrounds. Now, what about the areas in between? First of all, we need to determine these regions, which can be done by subtracting the `sure` foreground from the background:

```
sure_fg = np.uint8(sure_fg)
unknown = cv2.subtract(sure_bg,sure_fg)
```

Now that we have these areas, we can build our famous "barriers" to stop the water from merging. This is done with the `connectedComponents` function. We took a glimpse at the graph theory when we analyzed the GrabCut algorithm, and conceptualized an image as a set of nodes that are connected by edges. Given the sure foreground areas, some of these nodes will be connected together, but some won't. This means that they belong to different water valleys, and there should be a barrier between them:

```
ret, markers = cv2.connectedComponents(sure_fg)
```

Now we add 1 to the background areas because we only want unknowns to stay at 0:

```
markers = markers+1
markers[unknown==255] = 0
```

Finally, we open the gates! Let the water fall and our barriers be drawn in red:

```
markers = cv2.watershed(img,markers)
img[markers == -1] = [255,0,0]
plt.imshow(img)
plt.show()
```

Now, let's show the result:

Needless to say, I am now hungry!

Summary

In this chapter, we learned about gathering three-dimensional information from bi-dimensional input (a video frame or an image). Firstly, we examined depth cameras, and then epipolar geometry and stereo images, so we are now able to calculate disparity maps. Finally, we looked at image segmentation with two of the most popular methods: GrabCut and Watershed.

This chapter has introduced us to the world of interpreting information provided by images and we are now ready to explore another important feature of OpenCV: feature descriptors and keypoint detection.

5
Detecting and Recognizing Faces

Among the many reasons that make computer vision a fascinating subject is the fact that computer vision makes very *futuristic*-sounding tasks a reality. One such feature is face detection. OpenCV has a built-in facility to perform face detection, which has virtually infinite applications in the real world in all sorts of contexts, from security to entertainment.

This chapter introduces some of OpenCV's face detection functionalities, along with the data files that define particular types of trackable objects. Specifically, we look at Haar cascade classifiers, which analyze contrast between adjacent image regions to determine whether or not a given image or subimage matches a known type. We consider how to combine multiple Haar cascade classifiers in a hierarchy, such that one classifier identifies a parent region (for our purposes, a face) and other classifiers identify child regions (eyes, nose, and mouth).

We also take a detour into the humble but important subject of rectangles. By drawing, copying, and resizing rectangular image regions, we can perform simple manipulations on image regions that we are tracking.

By the end of this chapter, we will integrate face tracking and rectangle manipulations into Cameo. Finally, we'll have some face-to-face interaction!

Conceptualizing Haar cascades

When we talk about classifying objects and tracking their location, what exactly are we hoping to pinpoint? What constitutes a recognizable part of an object?

Photographic images, even from a webcam, may contain a lot of detail for our (human) viewing pleasure. However, image detail tends to be unstable with respect to variations in lighting, viewing angle, viewing distance, camera shake, and digital noise. Moreover, even real differences in physical detail might not interest us for the purpose of classification. I was taught in school that no two snowflakes look alike under a microscope. Fortunately, as a Canadian child, I had already learned how to recognize snowflakes without a microscope, as the similarities are more obvious in bulk.

Thus, some means of abstracting image detail is useful in producing stable classification and tracking results. The abstractions are called **features**, which are said to be **extracted** from the image data. There should be far fewer features than pixels, though any pixel might influence multiple features. The level of similarity between two images can be evaluated based on Euclidean distances between the images' corresponding features.

For example, distance might be defined in terms of spatial coordinates or color coordinates. Haar-like features are one type of feature that is often applied to real-time face tracking. They were first used for this purpose in the paper, *Robust Real-Time Face Detection, Paul Viola and Michael Jones, Kluwer Academic Publishers, 2001* (available at `http://www.vision.caltech.edu/html-files/EE148-2005-Spring/pprs/viola04ijcv.pdf`). Each Haar-like feature describes the pattern of contrast among adjacent image regions. For example, edges, vertices, and thin lines each generate distinctive features.

For any given image, the features may vary depending on the region's size; this may be called the **window size**. Two images that differ only in scale should be capable of yielding similar features, albeit for different window sizes. Thus, it is useful to generate features for multiple window sizes. Such a collection of features is called a **cascade**. We may say a Haar cascade is scale-invariant or, in other words, robust to changes in scale. OpenCV provides a classifier and tracker for scale-invariant Haar cascades that it expects to be in a certain file format.

Haar cascades, as implemented in OpenCV, are not robust to changes in rotation. For example, an upside-down face is not considered similar to an upright face and a face viewed in profile is not considered similar to a face viewed from the front. A more complex and more resource-intensive implementation could improve Haar cascades' robustness to rotation by considering multiple transformations of images as well as multiple window sizes. However, we will confine ourselves to the implementation in OpenCV.

Getting Haar cascade data

Once you have a copy of the source code of OpenCV 3, you will find a folder, `data/haarcascades`.

This folder contains all the XML files used by the OpenCV face detection engine to detect faces in still images, videos, and camera feeds.

Once you find `haarcascades`, create a directory for your project; in this folder, create a subfolder called `cascades`, and copy the following files from `haarcascades` into `cascades`:

```
haarcascade_profileface.xml
haarcascade_righteye_2splits.xml
haarcascade_russian_plate_number.xml
haarcascade_smile.xml
haarcascade_upperbody.xml
```

As their names suggest, these cascades are for tracking faces, eyes, noses, and mouths. They require a frontal, upright view of the subject. We will use them later when building a face detector. If you are curious about how these data sets are generated, refer to *Appendix B, Generating Haar Cascades for Custom Targets*. With a lot of patience and a powerful computer, you can make your own cascades and train them for various types of objects.

Using OpenCV to perform face detection

Unlike what you may think from the outset, performing face detection on a still image or a video feed is an extremely similar operation. The latter is just the sequential version of the former: face detection on videos is simply face detection applied to each frame read into the program from the camera. Naturally, a whole host of concepts are applied to video face detection such as tracking, which does not apply to still images, but it's always good to know that the underlying theory is the same.

So let's go ahead and detect some faces.

Performing face detection on a still image

The first and most basic way to perform face detection is to load an image and detect faces in it. To make the result visually meaningful, we will draw rectangles around faces on the original image.

Now that you have `haarcascades` included in your project, let's go ahead and create a basic script to perform face detection.

```
import cv2

filename = '/path/to/my/pic.jpg'

def detect(filename):
  face_cascade =
    cv2.CascadeClassifier('./cascades/
      haarcascade_frontalface_default.xml')

  img = cv2.imread(filename)
  gray = cv2.cvtColor(img, cv2.COLOR_BGR2GRAY)
  faces = face_cascade.detectMultiScale(gray, 1.3, 5)
  for (x,y,w,h) in faces:
    img = cv2.rectangle(img,(x,y),(x+w,y+h),(255,0,0),2)
  cv2.namedWindow('Vikings Detected!!')
  cv2.imshow('Vikings Detected!!', img)
  cv2.imwrite('./vikings.jpg', img)
  cv2.waitKey(0)

detect(filename)
```

Let's go through the code. First, we use the obligatory `cv2` import (you'll find that every script in this book will start like this, or almost similar). Secondly, we declare the `detect` function.

```
def detect(filename):
```

Within this function, we declare a `face_cascade` variable, which is a `CascadeClassifier` object for faces, and responsible for face detection.

```
face_cascade =
cv2.CascadeClassifier('./cascades/
  haarcascade_frontalface_default.xml')
```

We then load our file with cv2.imread, and convert it to grayscale, because that's the color space in which the face detection happens.

The next step (face_cascade.detectMultiScale) is where we operate the actual face detection.

```
img = cv2.imread(filename)
gray = cv2.cvtColor(img, cv2.COLOR_BGR2GRAY)
faces = face_cascade.detectMultiScale(gray, 1.3, 5)
```

The parameters passed are scaleFactor and minNeighbors, which determine the percentage reduction of the image at each iteration of the face detection process, and the minimum number of neighbors retained by each face rectangle at each iteration. This may all seem a little complex in the beginning but you can check all the options out in the official documentation.

The value returned from the detection operation is an array of tuples that represent the face rectangles. The utility method, cv2.rectangle, allows us to draw rectangles at the specified coordinates (x and y represent the left and top coordinates, w and h represent the width and height of the face rectangle).

We will draw blue rectangles around all the faces we find by looping through the faces variable, making sure we use the original image for drawing, not the gray version.

```
for (x,y,w,h) in faces:
    img = cv2.rectangle(img,(x,y),(x+w,y+h),(255,0,0),2)
```

Lastly, we create a namedWindow instance and display the resulting processed image in it. To prevent the image window from closing automatically, we insert a call to waitKey, which closes the window down at the press of any key.

```
cv2.namedWindow('Vikings Detected!!')
cv2.imshow('Vikings Detected!!', img)
cv2.waitKey(0)
```

And there we go, a whole set of Vikings have been detected in our image, as shown in the following screenshot:

Performing face detection on a video

We now have a good foundation to understand how to perform face detection on a still image. As mentioned previously, we can repeat the process on the individual frames of a video (be it a camera feed or a video) and perform face detection.

The script will perform the following tasks: it will open a camera feed, it will read a frame, it will examine that frame for faces, it will scan for eyes within the faces detected, and then it will draw blue rectangles around the faces and green rectangles around the eyes.

1. Let's create a file called `face_detection.py` and start by importing the necessary module:

```
import cv2
```

2. After this, we declare a method, `detect()`, which will perform face detection.

```
    def detect():
face_cascade =
  cv2.CascadeClassifier('./cascades/
    haarcascade_frontalface_default.xml')
eye_cascade =
  cv2.CascadeClassifier('./cascades/haarcascade_eye.xml')
camera = cv2.VideoCapture(0)
```

3. The first thing we need to do inside the `detect()` method is to load the Haar cascade files so that OpenCV can operate face detection. As we copied the cascade files in the local `cascades/` folder, we can use a relative path. Then, we open a `VideoCapture` object (the camera feed). The `VideoCapture` constructor takes a parameter, which indicates the camera to be used; `zero` indicates the first camera available.

```
while (True):
    ret, frame = camera.read()
    gray = cv2.cvtColor(frame, cv2.COLOR_BGR2GRAY)
```

4. Next up, we capture a frame. The `read()` method returns two values: a Boolean indicating the success of the frame read operation, and the frame itself. We capture the frame, and then we convert it to grayscale. This is a necessary operation, because face detection in OpenCV happens in the grayscale color space:

```
    faces = face_cascade.detectMultiScale(gray, 1.3, 5)
```

5. Much like the single still image example, we call `detectMultiScale` on the grayscale version of the frame.

```
    for (x,y,w,h) in faces:
        img =
            cv2.rectangle(frame,(x,y),(x+w,y+h),(255,0,0),
                2)


        roi_gray = gray[y:y+h, x:x+w]

        eyes = eye_cascade.detectMultiScale(roi_gray, 1.03,
            5, 0, (40,40))
```

There are a few additional parameters in the eye detection. Why? The method signature for detectMultiScale takes a number of optional parameters: in the case of detecting a face, the default options were good enough to detect faces. However, eyes are a smaller feature of the face, and self-casting shadows in my beard or my nose and random shadows in the frame were triggering **false positives**.

By limiting the search for eyes to a minimum size of 40x40 pixels, I was able to discard all false positives. Go ahead and test these parameters until you reach a point at which your application performs as you expected it to (for example, you can try and specify a maximum size for the feature too, or increase the scale factor and number of neighbors).

6. Here we have a further step compared to the still image example: we create a region of interest corresponding to the face rectangle, and within this rectangle, we operate "eye detection". This makes sense as you wouldn't want to go looking for eyes outside a face (well, for human beings at least!).

```
for (ex,ey,ew,eh) in eyes:
    cv2.rectangle(img,(ex,ey),(ex+ew,ey+eh),
        (0,255,0),2)
```

7. Again, we loop through the resulting eye tuples and draw green rectangles around them.

```
cv2.imshow("camera", frame)
if cv2.waitKey(1000 / 12) & 0xff == ord("q"):
    break

camera.release()
cv2.destroyAllWindows()

if __name__ == "__main__":
    detect()
```

8. Finally, we show the resulting frame in the window. All being well, if any face is within the field of view of the camera, you will have a blue rectangle around their face and a green rectangle around each eye, as shown in this screenshot:

Performing face recognition

Detecting faces is a fantastic feature of OpenCV and one that constitutes the basis for a more advanced operation: face recognition. What is face recognition? It's the ability of a program, given an image or a video feed, to identify a person. One of the ways to achieve this (and the approach adopted by OpenCV) is to "train" the program by feeding it a set of classified pictures (a facial database), and operate the recognition against those pictures.

This is the process that OpenCV and its face recognition module follow to recognize faces.

Another important feature of the face recognition module is that each recognition has a confidence score, which allows us to set thresholds in real-life applications to limit the amount of false reads.

Let's start from the very beginning; to operate face recognition, we need faces to recognize. You can do this in two ways: supply the images yourself or obtain freely available face databases. There are a number of face databases on the Internet:

- **The Yale face database (Yalefaces)**: `http://vision.ucsd.edu/content/yale-face-database`

- **The AT&T**: `http://www.cl.cam.ac.uk/research/dtg/attarchive/facedatabase.html`

- **The Extended Yale or Yale B**: `http://www.cl.cam.ac.uk/research/dtg/attarchive/facedatabase.html`

To operate face recognition on these samples, you would then have to run face recognition on an image that contains the face of one of the sampled people. That may be an educational process, but I found it to be not as satisfying as providing images of my own. In fact, I probably had the same thought that many people had: I wonder if I could write a program that recognizes my face with a certain degree of confidence.

Generating the data for face recognition

So let's go ahead and write a script that will generate those images for us. A few images containing different expressions are all that we need, but we have to make sure the sample images adhere to certain criteria:

- Images will be grayscale in the .pgm format
- Square shape
- All the same size images (I used 200 x 200; most freely available sets are smaller than that)

Here's the script itself:

```
import cv2

def generate():
  face_cascade = cv2.CascadeClassifier('./cascades/
    haarcascade_frontalface_default.xml')
```

```
eye_cascade =
  cv2.CascadeClassifier('./cascades/haarcascade_eye.xml')
camera = cv2.VideoCapture(0)
count = 0
while (True):
  ret, frame = camera.read()
  gray = cv2.cvtColor(frame, cv2.COLOR_BGR2GRAY)

  faces = face_cascade.detectMultiScale(gray, 1.3, 5)

  for (x,y,w,h) in faces:
      img = cv2.rectangle(frame,(x,y),(x+w,y+h),(255,0,0),2)

      f = cv2.resize(gray[y:y+h, x:x+w], (200, 200))

      cv2.imwrite('./data/at/jm/%s.pgm' % str(count), f)
      count += 1

  cv2.imshow("camera", frame)
  if cv2.waitKey(1000 / 12) & 0xff == ord("q"):
    break

  camera.release()
  cv2.destroyAllWindows()

if __name__ == "__main__":
  generate()
```

What is quite interesting about this exercise is that we are going to generate sample images building on our newfound knowledge of how to detect a face in a video feed. Effectively, what we are doing is detecting a face, cropping that region of the gray-scaled frame, resizing it to be 200x200 pixels, and saving it with a name in a particular folder (in my case, jm; you can use your initials) in the .pgm format.

I inserted a variable, count, because we needed progressive names for the images. Run the script for a few seconds, change expressions a few times, and check the destination folder you specified in the script. You will find a number of images of your face, grayed, resized, and named with the format, <count>.pgm.

Let's now move on to try and recognize our face in a video feed. This should be fun!

Recognizing faces

OpenCV 3 comes with three main methods for recognizing faces, based on three different algorithms: **Eigenfaces**, **Fisherfaces**, and **Local Binary Pattern Histograms** (LBPH). It is beyond the scope of this book to get into the nitty-gritty of the theoretical differences between these methods, but we can give a high-level overview of the concepts.

I will refer you to the following links for a detailed description of the algorithms:

- **Principal Component Analysis (PCA)**: A very intuitive introduction by Jonathon Shlens is available at `http://arxiv.org/pdf/1404.1100v1.pdf`. This algorithm was invented in 1901 by K. Pearson, and the original paper, *On Lines and Planes of Closest Fit to Systems of Points in Space*, is available at `http://stat.smmu.edu.cn/history/pearson1901.pdf`.

- **Eigenfaces**: The paper, *Eigenfaces for Recognition, M. Turk and A. Pentland, 1991*, is available at `http://www.cs.ucsb.edu/~mturk/Papers/jcn.pdf`.

- **Fisherfaces**: The seminal paper, *THE USE OF MULTIPLE MEASUREMENTS IN TAXONOMIC PROBLEMS, R.A. Fisher, 1936*, is available at `http://onlinelibrary.wiley.com/doi/10.1111/j.1469-1809.1936.tb02137.x/pdf`.

- **Local Binary Pattern**: The first paper describing this algorithm is *Performance evaluation of texture measures with classification based on Kullback discrimination of distributions, T. Ojala, M. Pietikainen, D. Harwood* and is available at `http://ieeexplore.ieee.org/xpl/articleDetails.jsp?arnumber=576366&searchWithin%5B%5D=%22Authors%22%3A.QT.Ojala%2C+T..QT.&newsearch=true`.

First and foremost, all methods follow a similar process; they all take a set of classified observations (our face database, containing numerous samples per individual), get "trained" on it, perform an analysis of faces detected in an image or video, and determine two elements: whether the subject is identified, and a measure of the confidence of the subject really being identified, which is commonly known as the confidence score.

Eigenfaces performs a so called PCA, which—of all the mathematical concepts you will hear mentioned in relation to computer vision—is possibly the most descriptive. It basically identifies principal components of a certain set of observations (again, your face database), calculates the **divergence** of the current observation (the faces being detected in an image or frame) compared to the dataset, and it produces a value. The smaller the value, the smaller the difference between face database and detected face; hence, a value of 0 is an exact match.

Fisherfaces derives from PCA and evolves the concept, applying more complex logic. While computationally more intensive, it tends to yield more accurate results than Eigenfaces.

LBPH instead roughly (again, from a very high level) divides a detected face into small cells and compares each cell to the corresponding cell in the model, producing a histogram of matching values for each area. Because of this flexible approach, LBPH is the only face recognition algorithm that allows the model sample faces and the detected faces to be of different shape and size. I personally found this to be the most accurate algorithm generally speaking, but each algorithm has its strengths and weaknesses.

Preparing the training data

Now that we have our data, we need to load these sample pictures into our face recognition algorithms. All face recognition algorithms take two parameters in their `train()` method: an array of images and an array of labels. What do these labels represent? They are the IDs of a certain individual/face so that when face recognition is performed, we not only know the person was recognized but also who—among the many people available in our database—the person is.

To do that, we need to create a **comma-separated value (CSV)** file, which will contain the path to a sample picture followed by the ID of that person. In my case, I have 20 pictures generated with the previous script, in the subfolder, `jm/`, of the folder, `data/at/`, which contains all the pictures of all the individuals.

My CSV file therefore looks like this:

```
jm/1.pgm;0
jm/2.pgm;0
jm/3.pgm;0
...
jm/20.pgm;0
```

 The dots are all the missing numbers. The `jm/` instance indicates the subfolder, and the `0` value at the end is the ID for my face.

OK, at this stage, we have everything we need to instruct OpenCV to recognize our face.

Loading the data and recognizing faces

Next up, we need to load these two resources (the array of images and CSV file) into the face recognition algorithm, so it can be trained to recognize our face. To do this, we build a function that reads the CSV file and—for each line of the file—loads the image at the corresponding path into the images array and the ID into the labels array.

```python
def read_images(path, sz=None):


    c = 0
    X,y = [], []
    for dirname, dirnames, filenames in os.walk(path):
        for subdirname in dirnames:
            subject_path = os.path.join(dirname, subdirname)
            for filename in os.listdir(subject_path):
                try:
                    if (filename == ".directory"):
                        continue
                    filepath = os.path.join(subject_path,
                        filename)
                    im = cv2.imread(os.path.join(subject_path,
                        filename), cv2.IMREAD_GRAYSCALE)

                    # resize to given size (if given)
                    if (sz is not None):
                        im = cv2.resize(im, (200, 200))

                    X.append(np.asarray(im, dtype=np.uint8))
                    y.append(c)
                except IOError, (errno, strerror):
                    print "I/O error({0}): {1}".format(errno,
                        strerror)
                except:
                    print "Unexpected error:", sys.exc_info()[0]
                    raise
            c = c+1


    return [X,y]
```

Performing an Eigenfaces recognition

We're ready to test the face recognition algorithm. Here's the script to perform it:

```
def face_rec():
    names = ['Joe', 'Jane', 'Jack']
    if len(sys.argv) < 2:
        print "USAGE: facerec_demo.py </path/to/images>
            [</path/to/store/images/at>]"
        sys.exit()

    [X,y] = read_images(sys.argv[1])
    y = np.asarray(y, dtype=np.int32)

    if len(sys.argv) == 3:
        out_dir = sys.argv[2]

    model = cv2.face.createEigenFaceRecognizer()
    model.train(np.asarray(X), np.asarray(y))
    camera = cv2.VideoCapture(0)
    face_cascade = cv2.CascadeClassifier('./cascades/
        haarcascade_frontalface_default.xml')
    while (True):
      read, img = camera.read()
      faces = face_cascade.detectMultiScale(img, 1.3, 5)
      for (x, y, w, h) in faces:
        img = cv2.rectangle(img,(x,y),(x+w,y+h),(255,0,0),2)
        gray = cv2.cvtColor(img, cv2.COLOR_BGR2GRAY)
        roi = gray[x:x+w, y:y+h]
        try:
            roi = cv2.resize(roi, (200, 200),
                interpolation=cv2.INTER_LINEAR)
            params = model.predict(roi)
            print "Label: %s, Confidence: %.2f" % (params[0],
                params[1])
            cv2.putText(img, names[params[0]], (x, y - 20),
                cv2.FONT_HERSHEY_SIMPLEX, 1, 255, 2)
        except:
            continue
      cv2.imshow("camera", img)
      if cv2.waitKey(1000 / 12) & 0xff == ord("q"):
        break
    cv2.destroyAllWindows()
```

There are a few lines that may look a bit mysterious, so let's analyze the script. First of all, there's an array of names declared; those are the actual names of the individual people I stored in my database of faces. It's great to identify a person as ID 0, but printing `'Joe'` on top of a face that's been correctly detected and recognized is much more dramatic.

So whenever the script recognizes an ID, we will print the corresponding name in the `names` array instead of an ID.

After this, we load the images as described in the previous function, create the face recognition model with `cv2.createEigenFaceRecognizer()`, and train it by passing the two arrays of images and labels (IDs). Note that the Eigenface recognizer takes two important parameters that you can specify: the first one is the number of principal components you want to keep and the second is a float value specifying a confidence threshold.

Next up, we repeat a similar process to the face detection operation. This time, though, we extend the processing of the frames by also operating face recognition on any face that's been detected.

This happens in two steps: firstly, we resize the detected face to the expected size (in my case, samples were 200x200 pixels), and then we call the `predict()` function on the resized region.

 This is a bit of a simplified process, and it serves the purpose of enabling you to have a basic application running and understand the process of face recognition in OpenCV 3. In reality, you will apply a few more optimizations, such as correctly aligning and rotating detected faces, so the accuracy of the recognition is maximized.

Lastly, we obtain the results of the recognition and, just for effect, we draw it in the frame:

Performing face recognition with Fisherfaces

What about Fisherfaces? The process doesn't change much; we simply need to instantiate a different algorithm. So, the declaration of our model variable would look like so:

```
model = cv2.face.createFisherFaceRecognizer()
```

Fisherface takes the same two arguments as Eigenfaces: the Fisherfaces to keep and the confidence threshold. Faces with confidence above this threshold will be discarded.

Performing face recognition with LBPH

Finally, let's take a quick look at the LBPH algorithm. Again, the process is very similar. However, the parameters taken by the algorithm factory are a bit more complex as they indicate in order: `radius`, `neighbors`, `grid_x`, `grid_y`, and the confidence threshold. If you don't specify these values, they will automatically be set to 1, 8, 8, 8, and 123.0. The model declaration will look like so:

```
model = cv2.face.createLBPHFaceRecognizer()
```

 Note that with LBPH, you won't need to resize images, as the division in grids allows comparing patterns identified in each cell.

Discarding results with confidence score

The `predict()` method returns a two-element array: the first element is the label of the recognized individual and the second is the confidence score. All algorithms come with the option of setting a confidence score threshold, which measures the distance of the recognized face from the original model, therefore a score of 0 signifies an exact match.

There may be cases in which you would rather retain all recognitions, and then apply further processing, so you can come up with your own algorithms to estimate the confidence score of a recognition; for example, if you are trying to identify people in a video, you may want to analyze the confidence score in subsequent frames to establish whether the recognition was successful or not. In this case, you can inspect the confidence score obtained by the algorithm and draw your own conclusions.

 The confidence score value is completely different in Eigenfaces/Fisherfaces and LBPH. Eigenfaces and Fisherfaces will produce values (roughly) in the range 0 to 20,000, with any score below 4-5,000 being quite a confident recognition.

LBPH works similarly; however, the reference value for a good recognition is below 50, and any value above 80 is considered as a low confidence score.

A normal custom approach would be to hold-off drawing a rectangle around a recognized face until we have a number of frames with a satisfying arbitrary confidence score, but you have total freedom to use OpenCV's face recognition module to tailor your application to your needs.

Summary

By now, you should have a good understanding of how face detection and face recognition work, and how to implement them in Python and OpenCV 3.

Face detection and face recognition are constantly evolving branches of computer vision, with algorithms being developed continuously, and they will evolve even faster in the near future with the emphasis posed on robotics and the Internet of things.

For now, the accuracy of detection and recognition heavily depends on the quality of the training data, so make sure you provide your applications with high-quality face databases and you will be satisfied with the results.

6
Retrieving Images and Searching Using Image Descriptors

Similar to the human eyes and brain, OpenCV can detect the main features of an image and extract these into so-called image descriptors. These features can then be used as a database, enabling image-based searches. Moreover, we can use keypoints to stitch images together and compose a bigger image (think of putting together many pictures to form a 360 degree panorama).

This chapter shows you how to detect features of an image with OpenCV and make use of them to match and search images. Throughout the chapter, we will take sample images and detect their main features, and then try to find a sample image contained in another image using homography.

Feature detection algorithms

There are a number of algorithms that can be used to detect and extract features, and we will explore most of them. The most common algorithms used in OpenCV are as follows:

- **Harris**: This algorithm is useful to detect corners
- **SIFT**: This algorithm is useful to detect blobs
- **SURF**: This algorithm is useful to detect blobs
- **FAST**: This algorithm is useful to detect corners
- **BRIEF**: This algorithm is useful to detect blobs
- **ORB**: This algorithm stands for **Oriented FAST and Rotated BRIEF**

Matching features can be performed with the following methods:

- Brute-Force matching
- FLANN-based matching

Spatial verification can then be performed with homography.

Defining features

What is a feature exactly? Why is a particular area of an image classifiable as a feature, while others are not? Broadly speaking, a feature is an area of interest in the image that is unique or easily recognizable. As you can imagine, corners and high-density areas are good features, while patterns that repeat themselves a lot or low-density areas (such as a blue sky) are not. Edges are good features as they tend to divide two regions of an image. A blob (an area of an image that greatly differs from its surrounding areas) is also an interesting feature.

Most feature detection algorithms revolve around the identification of corners, edges, and blobs, with some also focusing on the concept of a **ridge**, which you can conceptualize as the symmetry axis of an elongated object (think, for example, about identifying a road in an image).

Some algorithms are better at identifying and extracting features of a certain type, so it's important to know what your input image is so that you can utilize the best tool in your OpenCV belt.

Detecting features – corners

Let's start by identifying corners by utilizing `CornerHarris`, and let's do this with an example. If you continue studying OpenCV beyond this book, you'll find that—for many a reason—chessboards are a common subject of analysis in computer vision, partly because a chequered pattern is suited to many types of feature detections, and maybe because chess is pretty popular among geeks.

Here's our sample image:

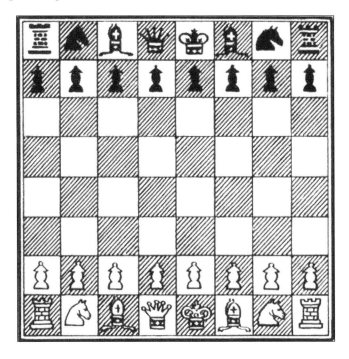

OpenCV has a very handy utility function called cornerHarris, which detects corners in an image. The code to illustrate this is incredibly simple:

```
import cv2
import numpy as np

img = cv2.imread('images/chess_board.png')
gray = cv2.cvtColor(img, cv2.COLOR_BGR2GRAY)
gray = np.float32(gray)
dst = cv2.cornerHarris(gray, 2, 23, 0.04)
img[dst>0.01 * dst.max()] = [0, 0, 255]
while (True):
  cv2.imshow('corners', img)
  if cv2.waitKey(1000 / 12) & 0xff == ord("q"):
    break
cv2.destroyAllWindows()
```

Let's analyze the code: after the usual imports, we load the chessboard image and turn it to grayscale so that `cornerHarris` can compute it. Then, we call the `cornerHarris` function:

```
dst = cv2.cornerHarris(gray, 2, 23, 0.04)
```

The most important parameter here is the third one, which defines the aperture of the Sobel operator. The Sobel operator performs the change detection in the rows and columns of an image to detect edges, and it does this using a kernel. The OpenCV `cornerHarris` function uses a Sobel operator whose aperture is defined by this parameter. In plain english, it defines how sensitive corner detection is. It must be between 3 and 31 and be an odd value. At value 3, all those diagonal lines in the black squares of the chessboard will register as corners when they touch the border of the square. At 23, only the corners of each square will be detected as corners.

Consider the following line:

```
img[dst>0.01 * dst.max()] = [0, 0, 255]
```

Here, in places where a red mark in the corners is detected, tweaking the second parameter in `cornerHarris` will change this, that is, the smaller the value, the smaller the marks indicating corners.

Here's the final result:

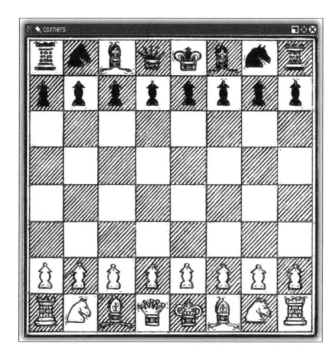

Great, we have corner points marked, and the result is meaningful at first glance; all the corners are marked in red.

Feature extraction and description using DoG and SIFT

The preceding technique, which uses `cornerHarris`, is great to detect corners and has a distinct advantage because corners are corners; they are detected even if the image is rotated.

However, if we reduce (or increase) the size of an image, some parts of the image may lose or even gain a corner quality.

For example, look at the following corner detections of the F1 Italian Grand Prix track:

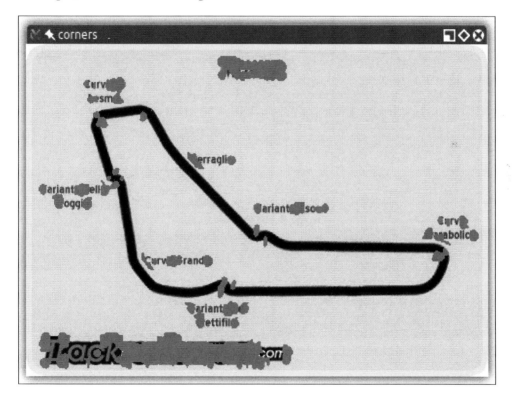

Here's a smaller version of the same screenshot:

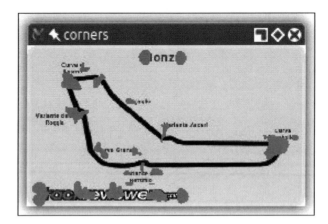

You will notice how corners are a lot more condensed; however, we didn't only gain corners, we also lost some! In particular, look at the **Variante Ascari** chicane that squiggles at the end of the NW/SE straight part of the track. In the larger version of the image, both the entrance and the apex of the double bend were detected as corners. In the smaller image, the apex is not detected as such. The more we reduce the image, the more likely it is that we're going to lose the entrance to that chicane too.

This loss of features raises an issue; we need an algorithm that will work regardless of the scale of the image. Enter **SIFT**: while **Scale-Invariant Feature Transform** may sound a bit mysterious, now that we know what problem we're trying to resolve, it actually makes sense. We need a function (a transform) that will detect features (a feature transform) and will not output different results depending on the scale of the image (a scale-invariant feature transform). Note that SIFT does not detect keypoints (which is done with Difference of Gaussians), but it describes the region surrounding them by means of a feature vector.

A quick introduction to **Difference of Gaussians (DoG)** is in order; we have already talked about low pass filters and blurring operations, specifically with the cv2. GaussianBlur() function. DoG is the result of different Gaussian filters applied to the same image. In *Chapter 3, Processing Images with OpenCV 3*, we applied this technique to compute a very efficient edge detection, and the idea is the same. The final result of a DoG operation contains areas of interest (keypoints), which are then going to be described through SIFT.

Let's see how SIFT behaves in an image full of corners and features:

Now, the beautiful panorama of Varese (Lombardy, Italy) also gains a computer vision meaning. Here's the code used to obtain this processed image:

```
import cv2
import sys
import numpy as np

imgpath = sys.argv[1]
img = cv2.imread(imgpath)

gray = cv2.cvtColor(img, cv2.COLOR_BGR2GRAY)

sift = cv2.xfeatures2d.SIFT_create()
keypoints, descriptor = sift.detectAndCompute(gray,None)

img = cv2.drawKeypoints(image=img, outImage=img, keypoints =
  keypoints, flags = cv2.DRAW_MATCHES_FLAGS_DRAW_RICH_KEYPOINT,
    color = (51, 163, 236))

cv2.imshow('sift_keypoints', img)
while (True):
  if cv2.waitKey(1000 / 12) & 0xff == ord("q"):
    break
cv2.destroyAllWindows()
```

After the usual imports, we load the image that we want to process. To make this script generic, we will take the image path as a command-line argument using the `sys` module of Python:

```
imgpath = sys.argv[1]
img = cv2.imread(imgpath)

gray = cv2.cvtColor(img, cv2.COLOR_BGR2GRAY)
```

We then turn the image into grayscale. At this stage, you may have gathered that most processing algorithms in Python need a grayscale feed in order to work.

The next step is to create a SIFT object and compute the grayscale image:

```
sift = cv2.xfeatures2d.SIFT_create()
keypoints, descriptor = sift.detectAndCompute(gray,None)
```

This is an interesting and important process; the SIFT object uses DoG to detect keypoints and computes a feature vector for the surrounding regions of each keypoint. As the name of the method clearly gives away, there are two main operations performed: detection and computation. The return value of the operation is a tuple containing keypoint information (keypoints) and the descriptor.

Finally, we process this image by drawing the keypoints on it and displaying it with the usual `imshow` function.

Note that in the `drawKeypoints` function, we pass a flag that has a value of 4. This is actually the `cv2` module property:

```
cv2.DRAW_MATCHES_FLAGS_DRAW_RICH_KEYPOINT
```

This code enables the drawing of circles and orientation of each keypoint.

Anatomy of a keypoint

Let's take a quick look at the definition, from the OpenCV documentation, of the keypoint class:

```
pt
size
angle
response
octave
class_id
```

Some properties are more self-explanatory than others, but let's not take anything for granted and go through each one:

- The `pt` (point) property indicates the *x* and *y* coordinates of the keypoint in the image.

- The `size` property indicates the diameter of the feature.

- The `angle` property indicates the orientation of the feature as shown in the preceding processed image.

- The `response` property indicates the strength of the keypoint. Some features are classified by SIFT as stronger than others, and `response` is the property you would check to evaluate the strength of a feature.

- The `octave` property indicates the layer in the pyramid where the feature was found. To fully explain this property, we would need to write an entire chapter on it, so I will only introduce the basic concept. The SIFT algorithm operates in a similar fashion to face detection algorithms in that, it processes the same image sequentially but alters the parameters of the computation.

  For example, the scale of the image and neighboring pixels are parameters that change at each iteration (`octave`) of the algorithm. So, the `octave` property indicates the layer at which the keypoint was detected.

- Finally, the object ID is the ID of the keypoint.

Feature extraction and detection using Fast Hessian and SURF

Computer vision is a relatively recent branch of computer science and many algorithms and techniques are of recent invention. SIFT is in fact only 16 years old, having been published by David Lowe in 1999.

SURF is a feature detection algorithm published in 2006 by Herbert Bay, which is several times faster than SIFT, and it is partially inspired by it.

 Note that both SIFT and SURF are patented algorithms and, for this reason, are made available in the `xfeatures2d` module of OpenCV.

It is not particularly relevant to this book to understand how SURF works under the hood, as much as we can use it in our applications and make the best of it. What is important to understand is that SURF is an OpenCV class that operates keypoint detection with the Fast Hessian algorithm and extraction with SURF, much like the SIFT class in OpenCV operating keypoint detection with DoG and extraction with SIFT.

Also, the good news is that as a feature detection algorithm, the API of SURF does not differ from SIFT. Therefore, we can simply edit the previous script to dynamically choose a feature detection algorithm instead of rewriting the entire program.

As we only support two algorithms for now, there is no need to find a particularly elegant solution to the evaluation of the algorithm to be used and we'll use the simple `if` blocks, as shown in the following code:

```
import cv2
import sys
import numpy as np

imgpath = sys.argv[1]
img = cv2.imread(imgpath)
alg = sys.argv[2]

def fd(algorithm):
  if algorithm == "SIFT":
    return cv2.xfeatures2d.SIFT_create()
  if algorithm == "SURF":
    return cv2.xfeatures2d.SURF_create(float(sys.argv[3]) if
      len(sys.argv) == 4 else 4000)

gray = cv2.cvtColor(img, cv2.COLOR_BGR2GRAY)

fd_alg = fd(alg)
keypoints, descriptor = fd_alg.detectAndCompute(gray,None)

img = cv2.drawKeypoints(image=img, outImage=img, keypoints =
  keypoints, flags = 4, color = (51, 163, 236))

cv2.imshow('keypoints', img)
while (True):
  if cv2.waitKey(1000 / 12) & 0xff == ord("q"):
    break
cv2.destroyAllWindows()
```

Here's the result using SURF with a threshold:

This image has been obtained by processing it with a SURF algorithm using a Hessian threshold of 8000. To be precise, I ran the following command:

```
> python feat_det.py images/varese.jpg SURF 8000
```

The higher the threshold, the less features identified, so play around with the values until you reach an optimal detection. In the preceding case, you can clearly see how individual buildings are detected as features.

In a process similar to the one we adopted in *Chapter 4*, *Depth Estimation and Segmentation*, when we were calculating disparity maps, try — as an exercise — to create a trackbar to feed the value of the Hessian threshold to the SURF instance, and see the number of features increase and decrease in an inversely proportional fashion.

Now, let's examine corner detection with FAST, the BRIEF keypoint descriptor, and ORB (which uses the two) and put feature detection to good use.

ORB feature detection and feature matching

If SIFT is young, and SURF younger, ORB is in its infancy. ORB was first published in 2011 as a fast alternative to SIFT and SURF.

The algorithm was published in the paper, *ORB: an efficient alternative to SIFT or SURF*, and is available in the PDF format at `http://www.vision.cs.chubu.ac.jp/CV-R/pdf/Rublee_iccv2011.pdf`.

ORB mixes techniques used in the FAST keypoint detection and the BRIEF descriptor, so it is definitely worth taking a quick look at FAST and BRIEF first. We will then talk about Brute-Force matching—one of the algorithms used for feature matching—and show an example of feature matching.

FAST

The **Features from Accelerated Segment Test (FAST)** algorithm works in a clever way; it draws a circle around including 16 pixels. It then marks each pixel brighter or darker than a particular threshold compared to the center of the circle. A corner is defined by identifying a number of contiguous pixels marked as brighter or darker.

FAST implements a high-speed test, which attempts at quickly skipping the whole 16-pixel test. To understand how this test works, let's take a look at this screenshot:

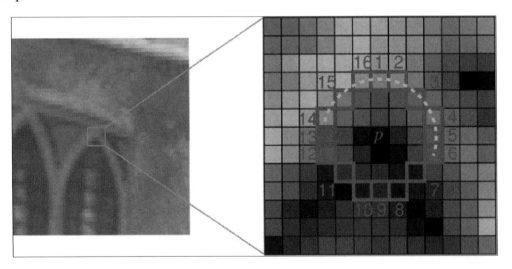

As you can see, three out of four of the test pixels (pixels number **1, 9, 5,** and **13**) must be within (or beyond) the threshold (and, therefore, marked as brighter or darker) and one must be in the opposite side of the threshold. If all four are marked as brighter or darker, or two are and two are not, the pixel is not a candidate corner.

FAST is an incredibly clever algorithm, but not devoid of weaknesses, and to compensate these weaknesses, developers analyzing images can implement a machine learning approach, feeding a set of images (relevant to your application) to the algorithm so that corner detection is optimized.

Despite this, FAST depends on a threshold, so the developer's input is always necessary (unlike SIFT).

BRIEF

Binary Robust Independent Elementary Features (BRIEF), on the other hand, is not a feature detection algorithm, but a descriptor. We have not yet explored this concept, so let's explain what a descriptor is, and then look at BRIEF.

You will notice that when we previously analyzed images with SIFT and SURF, the heart of the entire process is the call to the `detectAndCompute` function. This function operates two different steps: detection and computation, and they return two different results if coupled in a tuple.

The result of detection is a set of keypoints; the result of the computation is the descriptor. This means that the OpenCV's SIFT and SURF classes are both detectors and descriptors (although, remember that the original algorithms are not! OpenCV's SIFT is really DoG plus SIFT and OpenCV's SURF is really Fast Hessian plus SURF).

Keypoint descriptors are a representation of the image that serves as the gateway to feature matching because you can compare the keypoint descriptors of two images and find commonalities.

BRIEF is one of the fastest descriptors currently available. The theory behind BRIEF is actually quite complicated, but suffice to say that BRIEF adopts a series of optimizations that make it a very good choice for feature matching.

Brute-Force matching

A Brute-Force matcher is a descriptor matcher that compares two descriptors and generates a result that is a list of matches. The reason why it's called Brute-Force is that there is little optimization involved in the algorithm; all the features in the first descriptor are compared to the features in the second descriptor, and each comparison is given a distance value and the best result is considered a match.

This is why it's called Brute-Force. In computing, the term, **brute-force**, is often associated with an approach that prioritizes the exhaustion of all possible combinations (for example, all the possible combinations of characters to crack a password) over some clever and convoluted algorithmical logic. OpenCV provides a `BFMatcher` object that does just that.

Feature matching with ORB

Now that we have a general idea of what FAST and BRIEF are, we can understand why the team behind ORB (at the time composed by Ethan Rublee, Vincent Rabaud, Kurt Konolige, and Gary R. Bradski) chose these two algorithms as a foundation for ORB.

In their paper, the authors aim at achieving the following results:

- The addition of a fast and accurate orientation component to FAST
- The efficient computation of oriented BRIEF features
- Analysis of variance and correlation of oriented BRIEF features
- A learning method to decorrelate BRIEF features under rotational invariance, leading to better performance in nearest-neighbor applications.

Aside from very technical jargon, the main points are quite clear; ORB aims at optimizing and speeding up operations, including the very important step of utilizing BRIEF in a rotation-aware fashion so that matching is improved even in situations where a training image has a very different rotation to the query image.

At this stage, though, I bet you have had enough of the theory and want to sink your teeth in some feature matching, so let's go look at some code.

As an avid listener of music, the first example that comes to my mind is to get the logo of a band and match it to one of the band's albums:

```python
import numpy as np
import cv2
from matplotlib import pyplot as plt

img1 = cv2.imread('images/manowar_logo.png',cv2.IMREAD_GRAYSCALE)
img2 = cv2.imread('images/manowar_single.jpg',
  cv2.IMREAD_GRAYSCALE)

orb = cv2.ORB_create()
kp1, des1 = orb.detectAndCompute(img1,None)
kp2, des2 = orb.detectAndCompute(img2,None)
bf = cv2.BFMatcher(cv2.NORM_HAMMING, crossCheck=True)
matches = bf.match(des1,des2)
matches = sorted(matches, key = lambda x:x.distance)
img3 = cv2.drawMatches(img1,kp1,img2,kp2, matches[:40],
  img2,flags=2)
plt.imshow(img3),plt.show()
```

Let's now examine this code step by step.

After the usual imports, we load two images (the query image and the training image).

Note that you have probably seen the loading of images with a second parameter with the value of 0 being passed. This is because `cv2.imread` takes a second parameter that can be one of the following flags:

```
IMREAD_ANYCOLOR = 4
IMREAD_ANYDEPTH = 2
IMREAD_COLOR = 1
IMREAD_GRAYSCALE = 0
IMREAD_LOAD_GDAL = 8
IMREAD_UNCHANGED = -1
```

As you can see, `cv2.IMREAD_GRAYSCALE` is equal to `0`, so you can pass the flag itself or its value; they are the same thing.

This is the image we've loaded:

This is another image that we've loaded:

Now, we proceed to creating the ORB feature detector and descriptor:

```
orb = cv2.ORB_create()
kp1, des1 = orb.detectAndCompute(img1,None)
kp2, des2 = orb.detectAndCompute(img2,None)
```

In a similar fashion to what we did with SIFT and SURF, we detect and compute the keypoints and descriptors for both images.

The theory at this point is pretty simple; iterate through the descriptors and determine whether they are a match or not, and then calculate the quality of this match (distance) and sort the matches so that we can display the top *n* matches with a degree of confidence that they are, in fact, matching features on both images.

BFMatcher, as described in Brute-Force matching, does this for us:

```
bf = cv2.BFMatcher(cv2.NORM_HAMMING, crossCheck=True)
matches = bf.match(des1,des2)
matches = sorted(matches, key = lambda x:x.distance)
```

At this stage, we already have all the information we need, but as computer vision enthusiasts, we place quite a bit of importance on visually representing data, so let's draw these matches in a matplotlib chart:

```
img3 = cv2.drawMatches(img1,kp1,img2,kp2, matches[:40], img2,flags=2)
plt.imshow(img3),plt.show()
```

The result is as follows:

Using K-Nearest Neighbors matching

There are a number of algorithms that can be used to detect matches so that we can draw them. One of them is **K-Nearest Neighbors (KNN)**. Using different algorithms for different tasks can be really beneficial, because each algorithm has strengths and weaknesses. Some may be more accurate than others, some may be faster or less computationally expensive, so it's up to you to decide which one to use, depending on the task at hand.

For example, if you have hardware constraints, you may choose an algorithm that is less costly. If you're developing a real-time application, you may choose the fastest algorithm, regardless of how heavy it is on the processor or memory usage.

Among all the machine learning algorithms, KNN is probably the simplest, and while the theory behind it is interesting, it is well out of the scope of this book. Instead, we will simply show you how to use KNN in your application, which is not very different from the preceding example.

Crucially, the two points where the script differs to switch to KNN are in the way we calculate matches with the Brute-Force matcher, and the way we draw these matches. The preceding example, which has been edited to use KNN, looks like this:

```
import numpy as np
import cv2
from matplotlib import pyplot as plt

img1 = cv2.imread('images/manowar_logo.png',0)
img2 = cv2.imread('images/manowar_single.jpg',0)

orb = cv2.ORB_create()
kp1, des1 = orb.detectAndCompute(img1,None)
kp2, des2 = orb.detectAndCompute(img2,None)
bf = cv2.BFMatcher(cv2.NORM_HAMMING, crossCheck=True)
matches = bf.knnMatch(des1,des2, k=2)
img3 = cv2.drawMatchesKnn(img1,kp1,img2,kp2, matches,
  img2,flags=2)
plt.imshow(img3),plt.show()
```

The final result is somewhat similar to the previous one, so what is the difference between `match` and `knnMatch`? The difference is that `match` returns best matches, while KNN returns *k* matches, giving the developer the option to further manipulate the matches obtained with `knnMatch`.

For example, you could iterate through the matches and apply a ratio test so that you can filter out matches that do not satisfy a user-defined condition.

FLANN-based matching

Finally, we are going to take a look at **Fast Library for Approximate Nearest Neighbors (FLANN)**. The official Internet home of FLANN is at http://www.cs.ubc.ca/research/flann/.

Like ORB, FLANN has a more permissive license than SIFT or SURF, so you can freely use it in your project. Quoting the website of FLANN,

> *"FLANN is a library for performing fast approximate nearest neighbor searches in high dimensional spaces. It contains a collection of algorithms we found to work best for nearest neighbor search and a system for automatically choosing the best algorithm and optimum parameters depending on the dataset.*
>
> *FLANN is written in C++ and contains bindings for the following languages: C, MATLAB and Python."*

In other words, FLANN possesses an internal mechanism that attempts at employing the best algorithm to process a dataset depending on the data itself. FLANN has been proven to be 10 times times faster than other nearest neighbors search software.

FLANN is even available on GitHub at https://github.com/mariusmuja/flann. In my experience, I've found FLANN-based matching to be very accurate and fast as well as friendly to use.

Let's look at an example of FLANN-based feature matching:

```python
import numpy as np
import cv2
from matplotlib import pyplot as plt

queryImage = cv2.imread('images/bathory_album.jpg',0)
trainingImage = cv2.imread('images/vinyls.jpg',0)

# create SIFT and detect/compute
sift = cv2.xfeatures2d.SIFT_create()
kp1, des1 = sift.detectAndCompute(queryImage,None)
kp2, des2 = sift.detectAndCompute(trainingImage,None)

# FLANN matcher parameters
FLANN_INDEX_KDTREE = 0
indexParams = dict(algorithm = FLANN_INDEX_KDTREE, trees = 5)
```

```
searchParams = dict(checks=50)    # or pass empty dictionary

flann = cv2.FlannBasedMatcher(indexParams,searchParams)

matches = flann.knnMatch(des1,des2,k=2)

# prepare an empty mask to draw good matches
matchesMask = [[0,0] for i in xrange(len(matches))]

# David G. Lowe's ratio test, populate the mask
for i,(m,n) in enumerate(matches):
    if m.distance < 0.7*n.distance:
        matchesMask[i]=[1,0]

drawParams = dict(matchColor = (0,255,0),
                  singlePointColor = (255,0,0),
                  matchesMask = matchesMask,
                  flags = 0)

resultImage =
  cv2.drawMatchesKnn(queryImage,kp1,trainingImage,kp2,matches,
    None,**drawParams)

plt.imshow(resultImage,), plt.show()
```

Some parts of the preceding script will be familiar to you at this stage (import of modules, image loading, and creation of a SIFT object).

The interesting part is the declaration of the FLANN matcher, which follows the documentation at http://www.cs.ubc.ca/~mariusm/ uploads/FLANN/flann_manual-1.6.pdf.

We find that the FLANN matcher takes two parameters: an indexParams object and a searchParams object. These parameters, passed in a dictionary form in Python (and a struct in C++), determine the behavior of the index and search objects used internally by FLANN to compute the matches.

In this case, we could have chosen between `LinearIndex`, `KTreeIndex`, `KMeansIndex`, `CompositeIndex`, and `AutotuneIndex`, and we chose `KTreeIndex`. Why? This is because it's a simple enough index to configure (only requires the user to specify the number of kernel density trees to be processed; a good value is between 1 and 16) and clever enough (the kd-trees are processed in parallel). The `searchParams` dictionary only contains one field (checks) that specifies the number of times an index tree should be traversed. The higher the value, the longer it takes to compute the matching, but it will also be more accurate.

In reality, a lot depends on the input that you feed the program with. I've found that 5 kd-trees and 50 checks always yield a respectably accurate result, while only taking a short time to complete.

After the creation of the FLANN matcher and having created the matches array, matches are then filtered according to the test described by Lowe in his paper, *Distinctive Image Features from Scale-Invariant Keypoints*, available at `https://www.cs.ubc.ca/~lowe/papers/ijcv04.pdf`.

In its chapter, *Application to object recognition*, Lowe explains that not all matches are "good" ones, and that filtering according to an arbitrary threshold would not yield good results all the time. Instead, Dr. Lowe explains,

> *"The probability that a match is correct can be determined by taking the ratio of distance from the closest neighbor to the distance of the second closest."*

In the preceding example, discarding any value with a distance greater than 0.7 will result in just a few good matches being filtered out, while getting rid of around 90 percent of false matches.

Let's unveil the result of a practical example of FLANN. This is the query image that I've fed the script:

This is the training image:

Here, you may notice that the image contains the query image at position (5, 3) of this grid.

This is the FLANN processed result:

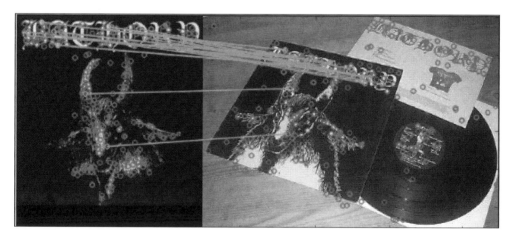

A perfect match!!

FLANN matching with homography

First of all, what is homography? Let's read a definition from the Internet:

> *"A relation between two figures, such that to any point of the one corresponds one and but one point in the other, and vise versa. Thus, a tangent line rolling on a circle cuts two fixed tangents of the circle in two sets of points that are homographic."*

If you—like me—are none the wiser from the preceding definition, you will probably find this explanation a bit clearer: homography is a condition in which two figures find each other when one is a perspective distortion of the other.

Unlike all the previous examples, let's first take a look at what we want to achieve so that we can fully understand what homography is. Then, we'll go through the code. Here's the final result:

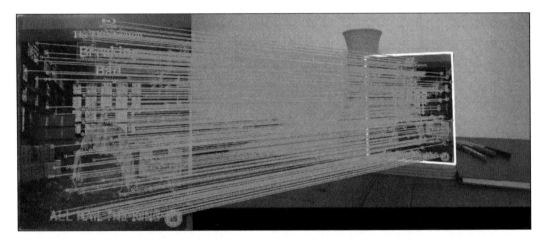

As you can see from the screenshot, we took a subject on the left, correctly identified in the image on the right-hand side, drew matching lines between keypoints, and even drew a white border showing the perspective deformation of the seed subject in the right-hand side of the image:

```python
import numpy as np
import cv2
from matplotlib import pyplot as plt

MIN_MATCH_COUNT = 10

img1 = cv2.imread('images/bb.jpg',0)
```

```
img2 = cv2.imread('images/color2_small.jpg',0)

sift = cv2.xfeatures2d.SIFT_create()
kp1, des1 = sift.detectAndCompute(img1,None)
kp2, des2 = sift.detectAndCompute(img2,None)


FLANN_INDEX_KDTREE = 0
index_params = dict(algorithm = FLANN_INDEX_KDTREE, trees = 5)
search_params = dict(checks = 50)


flann = cv2.FlannBasedMatcher(index_params, search_params)

matches = flann.knnMatch(des1,des2,k=2)

# store all the good matches as per Lowe's ratio test.
good = []
for m,n in matches:
    if m.distance < 0.7*n.distance:
        good.append(m)

if len(good)>MIN_MATCH_COUNT:
    src_pts = np.float32([ kp1[m.queryIdx].pt for m in good
        ]).reshape(-1,1,2)
    dst_pts = np.float32([ kp2[m.trainIdx].pt for m in good
        ]).reshape(-1,1,2)

    M, mask = cv2.findHomography(src_pts, dst_pts, cv2.RANSAC,5.0)
    matchesMask = mask.ravel().tolist()

    h,w = img1.shape
    pts = np.float32([ [0,0],[0,h-1],[w-1,h-1],[w-1,0]
        ]).reshape(-1,1,2)
    dst = cv2.perspectiveTransform(pts,M)

    img2 = cv2.polylines(img2,[np.int32(dst)],True,255,3,
        cv2.LINE_AA)

else:
    print "Not enough matches are found - %d/%d" %
        (len(good),MIN_MATCH_COUNT)
    matchesMask = None

draw_params = dict(matchColor = (0,255,0), # draw matches in green
    color
                   singlePointColor = None,
```

```
                           matchesMask = matchesMask, # draw only inliers
                           flags = 2)

    img3 = cv2.drawMatches(img1,kp1,img2,kp2,good,None,**draw_params)

    plt.imshow(img3, 'gray'),plt.show()
```

When compared to the previous FLANN-based matching example, the only difference (and this is where all the action happens) is in the `if` block.

Here's what happens in this code step by step: firstly, we make sure that we have at least a certain number of good matches (the minimum required to compute a homography is four), which we will arbitrarily set at 10 (in real life, you would probably use a higher value than this):

```
    if len(good) >MIN_MATCH_COUNT:
```

Then, we find the keypoints in the original image and the training image:

```
    src_pts = np.float32([ kp1[m.queryIdx].pt for m in good
        ]).reshape(-1,1,2)
    dst_pts = np.float32([ kp2[m.trainIdx].pt for m in good
        ]).reshape(-1,1,2)
```

Now, we find the homography:

```
    M, mask = cv2.findHomography(src_pts, dst_pts, cv2.RANSAC,5.0)
    matchesMask = mask.ravel().tolist()
```

Note that we create `matchesMask`, which will be used in the final drawing of the matches so that only points lying within the homography will have matching lines drawn.

At this stage, we simply have to calculate the perspective distortion of the original object into the second picture so that we can draw the border:

```
    h,w = img1.shape
    pts = np.float32([ [0,0], [0,h-1], [w-1,h-1], [w-1,0] ]).reshape(-
        1,1,2)
    dst = cv2.perspectiveTransform(pts,M)
    img2 = cv2.polylines(img2,[np.int32(dst)],True,255,3, cv2.LINE_AA)
```

And we then proceed to draw as per all our previous examples.

A sample application – tattoo forensics

Let's conclude this chapter with a real-life (or kind of) example. Imagine that you're working for the Gotham forensics department and you need to identify a tattoo. You have the original picture of the tattoo (imagine this coming from a CCTV footage) belonging to a criminal, but you don't know the identity of the person. However, you possess a database of tattoos, indexed with the name of the person to whom the tattoo belongs.

So, let's divide the task in two parts: save image descriptors to files first, and then, scan these for matches against the picture we are using as a query image.

Saving image descriptors to file

The first thing we will do is save image descriptors to an external file. This is so that we don't have to recreate the descriptors every time we want to scan two images for matches and homography.

In our application, we will scan a folder for images and create the corresponding descriptor files so that we have them readily available for future searches.

To create descriptors and save them to a file, we will use a process we have used a number of times in this chapter, namely load an image, create a feature detector, detect, and compute:

```
# generate_descriptors.py
import cv2
import numpy as np
from os import walk
from os.path import join
import sys

def create_descriptors(folder):
  files = []
  for (dirpath, dirnames, filenames) in walk(folder):
    files.extend(filenames)
  for f in files:
    save_descriptor(folder, f, cv2.xfeatures2d.SIFT_create())

def save_descriptor(folder, image_path, feature_detector):
  img = cv2.imread(join(folder, image_path), 0)
  keypoints, descriptors = feature_detector.detectAndCompute(img,
    None)
  descriptor_file = image_path.replace("jpg", "npy")
```

```
    np.save(join(folder, descriptor_file), descriptors)

  dir = sys.argv[1]

  create_descriptors(dir)
```

In this script, we pass the folder name where all our images are contained, and then create all the descriptor files in the same folder.

NumPy has a very handy `save()` utility, which dumps array data into a file in an optimized way. To generate the descriptors in the folder containing your script, run this command:

```
> python generate_descriptors.py <folder containing images>
```

Note that `cPickle/pickle` are more popular libraries for Python object serialization. However, in this particular context, we are trying to limit ourselves to the usage of OpenCV and Python with NumPy and SciPy.

Scanning for matches

Now that we have descriptors saved to files, all we need to do is to repeat the homography process on all the descriptors and find a potential match to our query image.

This is the process we will put in place:

- Loading a query image and creating a descriptor for it (`tattoo_seed.jpg`)
- Scanning the folder with descriptors
- For each descriptor, computing a FLANN-based match
- If the number of matches is beyond an arbitrary threshold, including the file of potential culprits (remember we're investigating a crime)
- Of all the culprits, electing the one with the highest number of matches as the potential suspect

Let's inspect the code to achieve this:

```
from os.path import join
from os import walk
import numpy as np
import cv2
from sys import argv

# create an array of filenames
```

```
folder = argv[1]
query = cv2.imread(join(folder, "tattoo_seed.jpg"), 0)

# create files, images, descriptors globals
files = []
images = []
descriptors = []
for (dirpath, dirnames, filenames) in walk(folder):
  files.extend(filenames)
  for f in files:
    if f.endswith("npy") and f != "tattoo_seed.npy":
      descriptors.append(f)
  print descriptors

# create the sift detector
sift = cv2.xfeatures2d.SIFT_create()
query_kp, query_ds = sift.detectAndCompute(query, None)

# create FLANN matcher
FLANN_INDEX_KDTREE = 0
index_params = dict(algorithm = FLANN_INDEX_KDTREE, trees = 5)
search_params = dict(checks = 50)
flann = cv2.FlannBasedMatcher(index_params, search_params)

# minimum number of matches
MIN_MATCH_COUNT = 10

potential_culprits = {}

print ">> Initiating picture scan..."
for d in descriptors:
  print "--------- analyzing %s for matches ------------" % d
  matches = flann.knnMatch(query_ds, np.load(join(folder, d)), k
    =2)
  good = []
  for m,n in matches:
      if m.distance < 0.7*n.distance:
          good.append(m)
  if len(good) > MIN_MATCH_COUNT:
    print "%s is a match! (%d)" % (d, len(good))
  else:
    print "%s is not a match" % d
```

```
      potential_culprits[d] = len(good)

  max_matches = None
  potential_suspect = None
  for culprit, matches in potential_culprits.iteritems():
    if max_matches == None or matches > max_matches:
      max_matches = matches
      potential_suspect = culprit

  print "potential suspect is %s" % potential_suspect.replace("npy",
    "").upper()
```

I saved this script as `scan_for_matches.py`. The only element of novelty in this script is the use of `numpy.load(filename)`, which loads an npy file into an np array.

Running the script produces the following output:

```
>> Initiating picture scan...
--------- analyzing posion-ivy.npy for matches -----------
posion-ivy.npy is not a match
--------- analyzing bane.npy for matches -----------
bane.npy is not a match
--------- analyzing two-face.npy for matches -----------
two-face.npy is not a match
--------- analyzing riddler.npy for matches -----------
riddler.npy is not a match
--------- analyzing penguin.npy for matches -----------
penguin.npy is not a match
--------- analyzing dr-hurt.npy for matches -----------
dr-hurt.npy is a match! (298)
--------- analyzing hush.npy for matches -----------
hush.npy is a match! (301)
potential suspect is HUSH.
```

If we were to represent this graphically, this is what we would see:

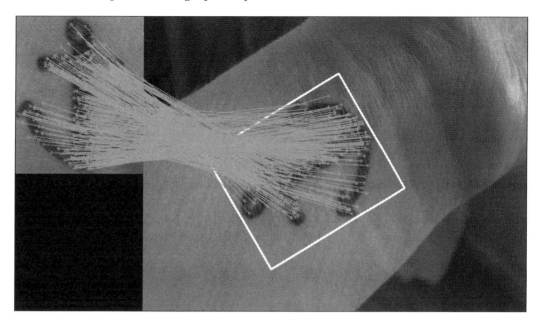

Summary

In this chapter, we learned about detecting features in images and extracting them into descriptors. We explored a number of algorithms available in OpenCV to accomplish this task, and then applied them to real-life scenarios to understand a real-world application of the concepts we explored.

We are now familiar with the concept of detecting features in an image (or a video frame), which is a good foundation for the next chapter.

7
Detecting and Recognizing Objects

This chapter will introduce the concept of detecting and recognizing objects, which is one of the most common challenges in computer vision. You've come this far in the book, so at this stage, you're wondering how far are you from mounting a computer in your car that will give you information about cars and people surrounding you through the use of a camera. Well, You're not too far from your goal, actually.

In this chapter, we will expand on the concept of object detection, which we initially explored when talking about recognizing faces, and adapt it to all sorts of real-life objects, not just faces.

Object detection and recognition techniques

We made a distinction in *Chapter 5, Detecting and Recognizing Faces*, which we'll reiterate for clarity: detecting an object is the ability of a program to determine if a certain region of an image contains an unidentified object, and recognizing is the ability of a program to identify this object. Recognizing normally only occurs in areas of interest where an object has been detected, for example, we have attempted to recognize faces on the areas of an image that contained a face in the first place.

When it comes to recognizing and detecting objects, there are a number of techniques used in computer vision, which we'll be examining:

- Histogram of Oriented Gradients
- Image pyramids
- Sliding windows

Unlike feature detection algorithms, these are not mutually exclusive techniques, rather, they are complimentary. You can perform a **Histogram of Oriented Gradients (HOG)** while applying the sliding windows technique.

So, let's take a look at HOG first and understand what it is.

HOG descriptors

HOG is a feature descriptor, so it belongs to the same family of algorithms, such as SIFT, SURF, and ORB.

It is used in image and video processing to detect objects. Its internal mechanism is really clever; an image is divided into portions and a gradient for each portion is calculated. We've observed a similar approach when we talked about face recognition through LBPH.

HOG, however, calculates histograms that are not based on color values, rather, they are based on gradients. As HOG is a feature descriptor, it is capable of delivering the type of information that is vital for feature matching and object detection/recognition.

Before diving into the technical details of how HOG works, let's first take a look at how HOG *sees* the world; here is an image of a truck:

This is its HOG version:

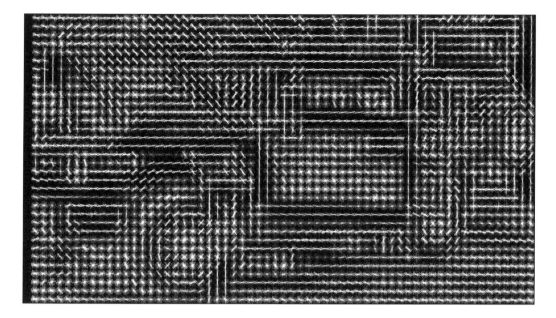

You can easily recognize the wheels and the main structure of the vehicle. So, what is HOG *seeing*? First of all, you can see how the image is divided into cells; these are 16x16 pixels cells. Each cell contains a visual representation of the calculated gradients of color in eight directions (N, NW, W, SW, S, SE, E, and NE).

These eight values contained in each cell are the famous histograms. Therefore, a single cell gets a unique *signature*, which you can mentally visualize to be somewhat like this:

The extrapolation of histograms into descriptors is quite a complex process. First, local histograms for each cell are calculated. The cells are grouped into larger regions called blocks. These blocks can be made of any number of cells, but Dalal and Triggs found that 2x2 cell blocks yielded the best results when performing people detection. A block-wide vector is created so that it can be normalized, accounting for variations in illumination and shadowing (a single cell is too small a region to detect such variations). This improves the accuracy of detection as it reduces the illumination and shadowing difference between the sample and the block being examined.

Simply comparing cells in two images would not work unless the images are identical (both in terms of size and data).

There are two main problems to resolve:

- Location
- Scale

The scale issue

Imagine, for example, if your sample was a detail (say, a bike) extrapolated from a larger image, and you're trying to compare the two pictures. You would not obtain the same gradient signatures and the detection would fail (even though the bike is in both pictures).

The location issue

Once we've resolved the scale problem, we have another obstacle in our path: a potentially detectable object can be anywhere in the image, so we need to scan the entire image in portions to make sure we can identify areas of interest, and within these areas, try to detect objects. Even if a sample image and object in the image are of identical size, there needs to be a way to instruct OpenCV to locate this object. So, the rest of the image is discarded and a comparison is made on potentially matching regions.

To obviate these problems, we need to familiarize ourselves with the concepts of image pyramid and sliding windows.

Image pyramid

Many of the algorithms used in computer vision utilize a concept called **pyramid**.

An image pyramid is a multiscale representation of an image. This diagram should help you understand this concept:

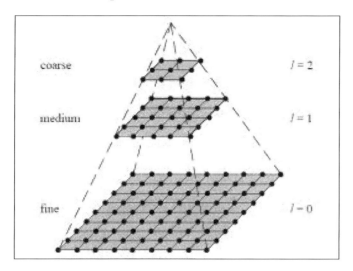

A multiscale representation of an image, or an image pyramid, helps you resolve the problem of detecting objects at different scales. The importance of this concept is easily explained through real-life hard facts, such as it is extremely unlikely that an object will appear in an image at the exact scale it appeared in our sample image.

Moreover, you will learn that object classifiers (utilities that allow you to detect objects in OpenCV) need *training*, and this training is provided through image databases made up of positive matches and negative matches. Among the positives, it is again unlikely that the object we want to identify will appear in the same scale throughout the training dataset.

We've got it, Joe. We need to take scale out of the equation, so now let's examine how an image pyramid is built.

An image pyramid is built through the following process:

1. Take an image.
2. Resize (smaller) the image using an arbitrary scale parameter.
3. Smoothen the image (using Gaussian blurring).
4. If the image is larger than an arbitrary minimum size, repeat the process from step 1.

Despite exploring image pyramids, scale ratio, and minimum sizes only at this stage of the book, you've already dealt with them. If you recall *Chapter 5, Detecting and Recognizing Faces,* we used the `detectMultiScale` method of the `CascadeClassifier` object.

Straight away, `detectMultiScale` doesn't sound so obscure anymore; in fact, it has become self-explanatory. The cascade classifier object attempts at detecting an object at different scales of an input image. The second piece of information that should become much clearer is the `scaleFactor` parameter of the `detectMultiScale()` method. This parameter represents the ratio at which the image will be resampled to a smaller size at each step of the pyramid.

The smaller the `scaleFactor` parameter, the more layers in the pyramid, and the slower and more computationally intensive the operation will be, although—to an extent—more accurate in results.

So, by now, you should have an understanding of what an image pyramid is, and why it is used in computer vision. Let's now move on to sliding windows.

Sliding windows

Sliding windows is a technique used in computer vision that consists of examining the shifting portions of an image (sliding windows) and operating detection on those using image pyramids. This is done so that an object can be detected at a multiscale level.

Sliding windows resolves location issues by scanning smaller regions of a larger image, and then repeating the scanning on different scales of the same image.

With this technique, each image is decomposed into portions, which allows discarding portions that are unlikely to contain objects, while the remaining portions are classified.

There is one problem that emerges with this approach, though: **overlapping regions**.

Let's expand a little bit on this concept to clarify the nature of the problem. Say, you're operating face detection on an image and are using sliding windows.

Each window slides off a few pixels at a time, which means that a sliding window happens to be a positive match for the same face in four different positions. Naturally, we don't want to report four matches, rather only one; furthermore, we're not interested in the portion of the image with a good score, but simply in the portion with the highest score.

Here's where non-maximum suppression comes into play: given a set of overlapping regions, we can suppress all the regions that are not classified with the maximum score.

Non-maximum (or non-maxima) suppression

Non-maximum (or non-maxima) suppression is a technique that suppresses all the results that relate to the same area of an image, which are not the maximum score for a particular area. This is because similarly colocated windows tend to have higher scores and overlapping areas are significant, but we are only interested in the window with the best result, and discarding overlapping windows with lower scores.

When examining an image with sliding windows, you want to make sure to retain the best window of a bunch of windows, all overlapping around the same subject.

To do this, you determine that all the windows with more than a threshold, x, in common will be thrown into the non-maximum suppression operation.

This is quite complex, but it's also not the end of this process. Remember the image pyramid? We're scanning the image at smaller scales iteratively to make sure to detect objects in different scales.

This means that you will obtain a series of windows at different scales, then, compute the size of a window obtained in a smaller scale as if it were detected in the original scale, and, finally, throw this window into the original mix.

It does sound a bit complex. Thankfully, we're not the first to come across this problem, which has been resolved in several ways. The fastest algorithm in my experience was implemented by Dr. Tomasz Malisiewicz at `http://www.computervisionblog.com/2011/08/blazing-fast-nmsm-from-exemplar-svm.html`. The example is in MATLAB, but in the application example, we will obviously use a Python version of it.

The general approach behind non-maximum suppression is as follows:

1. Once an image pyramid has been constructed, scan the image with the sliding window approach for object detection.
2. Collect all the current windows that have returned a positive result (beyond a certain arbitrary threshold), and take a window, `w`, with the highest response.
3. Eliminate all windows that overlap `w` significantly.
4. Move on to the next window with the highest response and repeat the process for the current scale.

When this process is complete, move up the next scale in the image pyramid and repeat the preceding process. To make sure windows are correctly represented at the end of the entire non-maximum suppression process, be sure to compute the window size in relation to the original size of the image (for example, if you detect a window at 50 percent scale of the original size in the pyramid, the detected window will actually be four times the size in the original image).

At the end of this process, you will have a set of maximum scored windows. Optionally, you can check for windows that are entirely contained in other windows (like we did for the people detection process at the beginning of the chapter) and eliminate those.

Now, how do we determine the score of a window? We need a classification system that determines whether a certain feature is present or not and a confidence score for this classification. This is where **support vector machines (SVM)** comes into play.

Support vector machines

Explaining in detail what an SVM is and does is beyond the scope of this book, but suffice it to say, SVM is an algorithm that—given labeled training data–enables the classification of this data by outputting an optimal *hyperplane*, which, in plain English, is the optimal plane that divides differently classified data. A visual representation will help you understand this:

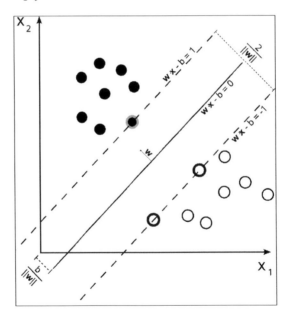

Why is it so helpful in computer vision and object detection in particular? This is due to the fact that finding the optimal division line between pixels that belong to an object and those that don't is a vital component of object detection.

The SVM model has been around since the early 1960s; however, the current form of its implementation originates in a 1995 paper by Corinna Cortes and Vadimir Vapnik, which is available at `http://link.springer.com/article/10.1007/BF00994018`.

Now that we have a good understanding of the concepts involved in object detection, we can start looking at a few examples. We will start from built-in functions and evolve into training our own custom object detectors.

People detection

OpenCV comes with `HOGDescriptor` that performs people detection.

Here's a pretty straightforward example:

```
import cv2
import numpy as np

def is_inside(o, i):
    ox, oy, ow, oh = o
    ix, iy, iw, ih = i
    return ox > ix and oy > iy and ox + ow < ix + iw and oy + oh <
        iy + ih

def draw_person(image, person):
  x, y, w, h = person
  cv2.rectangle(img, (x, y), (x + w, y + h), (0, 255, 255), 2)

img = cv2.imread("../images/people.jpg")
hog = cv2.HOGDescriptor()
hog.setSVMDetector(cv2.HOGDescriptor_getDefaultPeopleDetector())

found, w = hog.detectMultiScale(img)

found_filtered = []
for ri, r in enumerate(found):
    for qi, q in enumerate(found):
        if ri != qi and is_inside(r, q):
            break
    else:
```

```
            found_filtered.append(r)

    for person in found_filtered:
      draw_person(img, person)

    cv2.imshow("people detection", img)
    cv2.waitKey(0)
    cv2.destroyAllWindows()
```

After the usual imports, we define two very simple functions: `is_inside` and `draw_person`, which perform two minimal tasks, namely, determining whether a rectangle is fully contained in another rectangle, and drawing rectangles around detected people.

We then load the image and create `HOGDescriptor` through a very simple and self-explanatory code:

```
    cv2.HOGDescriptor()
```

After this, we specify that `HOGDescriptor` will use a default people detector.

This is done through the `setSVMDetector()` method, which—after our introduction to SVM—sounds less obscure than it may have if we hadn't introduced SVMs.

Next, we apply `detectMultiScale` on the loaded image. Interestingly, unlike all the face detection algorithms, we don't need to convert the original image to grayscale before applying any form of object detection.

The detection method will return an array of rectangles, which would be a good enough source of information for us to start drawing shapes on the image. If we did this, however, you would notice something strange: some of the rectangles are entirely contained in other rectangles. This clearly indicates an error in detection, and we can safely assume that a rectangle entirely inside another one can be discarded.

This is precisely the reason why we defined an `is_inside` function, and why we iterate through the result of the detection to discard false positives.

If you run the script yourself, you will see rectangles around people in the image.

Creating and training an object detector

Using built-in features makes it easy to come up with a quick prototype for an application, and we're all very grateful to the OpenCV developers for making great features, such as face detection or people detection readily available (truly, we are).

However, whether you are a hobbyist or a computer vision professional, it's unlikely that you will only deal with people and faces.

Moreover, if you're like me, you wonder how the people detector feature was created in the first place and if you can improve it. Furthermore, you may also wonder whether you can apply the same concepts to detect the most diverse type of objects, ranging from cars to goblins.

In an enterprise environment, you may have to deal with very specific detection, such as registration plates, book covers, or whatever your company may deal with.

So, the question is, how do we come up with our own classifiers?

The answer lies in SVM and bag-of-words technique.

We've already talked about HOG and SVM, so let's take a closer look at bag-of-words.

Bag-of-words

Bag-of-words (BOW) is a concept that was not initially intended for computer vision, rather, we use an evolved version of this concept in the context of computer vision. So, let's first talk about its basic version, which—as you may have guessed— originally belongs to the field of language analysis and information retrieval.

BOW is the technique by which we assign a count weight to each word in a series of documents; we then rerepresent these documents with vectors that represent these set of counts. Let's look at an example:

- **Document 1**: `I like OpenCV and I like Python`
- **Document 2**: `I like C++ and Python`
- **Document 3**: `I don't like artichokes`

These three documents allow us to build a dictionary (or codebook) with these values:

```
{
    I: 4,
    like: 4,
    OpenCV: 2,
    and: 2,
    Python: 2,
    C++: 1,
    dont: 1,
    artichokes: 1
}
```

We have eight entries. Let's now rerepresent the original documents using eight-entry vectors, each vector containing all the words in the dictionary with values representing the count for each term in the document. The vector representation of the preceding three sentences is as follows:

```
[2, 2, 1, 1, 1, 0, 0, 0]
[1, 1, 0, 1, 1, 1, 0, 0]
[1, 1, 0, 0, 0, 0, 1, 1]
```

This kind of representation of documents has many effective applications in the real world, such as spam filtering.

These vectors can be conceptualized as a histogram representation of documents or as a feature (the same way we extracted features from images in previous chapters), which can be used to train classifiers.

Now that we have a grasp of the basic concept of BOW or **bag of visual words** (**BOVW**) in computer vision, let's see how this applies to the world of computer vision.

BOW in computer vision

We are by now familiar with the concept of image features. We've used feature extractors, such as SIFT, and SURF, to extract features from images so that we could match these features in another image.

We've also familiarized ourselves with the concept of codebook, and we know about SVM, a model that can be fed a set of features and utilizes complex algorithms to classify train data, and can predict the classification of new data.

So, the implementation of a BOW approach will involve the following steps:

1. Take a sample dataset.
2. For each image in the dataset, extract descriptors (with SIFT, SURF, and so on).
3. Add each descriptor to the BOW trainer.
4. Cluster the descriptors to *k* clusters (okay, this sounds obscure, but bear with me) whose centers (centroids) are our visual words.

At this point, we have a dictionary of visual words ready to be used. As you can imagine, a large dataset will help make our dictionary richer in visual words. Up to an extent, the more words, the better!

After this, we are ready to test our classifier and attempt detection. The good news is that the process is very similar to the one outlined previously: given a test image, we can extract features and quantize them based on their distance to the nearest centroid to form a histogram.

Based on this, we can attempt to recognize visual words and locate them in the image. Here's a visual representation of the BOW process:

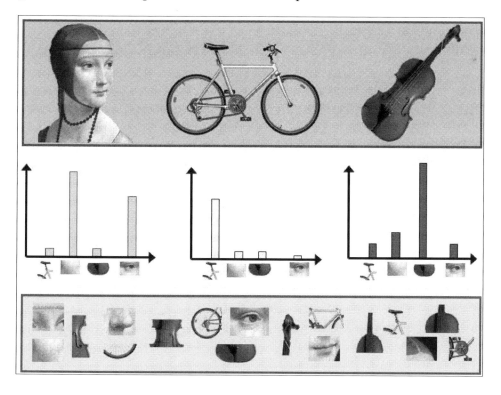

This is the point in the chapter when you have built an appetite for a practical example, and are rearing to code. However, before proceeding, I feel that a quick digression into the theory of the k-means clustering is necessary so that you can fully understand how visual words are created, and gain a better understanding of the process of object detection using BOW and SVM.

The k-means clustering

The k-means clustering is a method of vector quantization to perform data analysis. Given a dataset, *k* represents the number of clusters in which the dataset is going to be divided. The term "means" refers to the mathematical concept of mean, which is pretty basic, but for the sake of clarity, it's what people commonly refer to as average; when visually represented, the mean of a cluster is its **centroid** or the geometrical center of points in the cluster.

 Clustering refers to the grouping of points in a dataset into clusters.

One of the classes we will be using to perform object detection is called `BagOfWordsKMeansTrainer`; by now, you should able to deduce what the responsibility of this class is to create:

"`kmeans()` -based class to train a visual vocabulary using the bag-of-words approach"

This is as per the OpenCV documentation.

Here's a representation of a k-means clustering operation with five clusters:

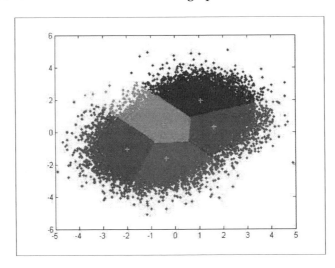

After this long theoretical introduction, we can look at an example, and start training our object detector.

Detecting cars

There is no virtual limit to the type of objects you can detect in your images and videos. However, to obtain an acceptable level of accuracy, you need a sufficiently large dataset, containing train images that are identical in size.

This would be a time consuming operation if we were to do it all by ourselves (which is entirely possible).

We can avail of ready-made datasets; there are a number of them freely downloadable from various sources:

- **The University of Illinois**: http://l2r.cs.uiuc.edu/~cogcomp/Data/Car/CarData.tar.gz

- **Stanford University**: http://ai.stanford.edu/~jkrause/cars/car_dataset.html

 Note that training images and test images are available in separate files.

I'll be using the UIUC dataset in my example, but feel free to explore the Internet for other types of datasets.

Now, let's take a look at an example:

```
import cv2
import numpy as np
from os.path import join

datapath = "/home/d3athmast3r/dev/python/CarData/TrainImages/"
def path(cls,i):
  return "%s/%s%d.pgm"  % (datapath,cls,i+1)

pos, neg = "pos-", "neg-"

detect = cv2.xfeatures2d.SIFT_create()
```

```
extract = cv2.xfeatures2d.SIFT_create()

flann_params = dict(algorithm = 1, trees = 5)flann =
  cv2.FlannBasedMatcher(flann_params, {})

bow_kmeans_trainer = cv2.BOWKMeansTrainer(40)
extract_bow = cv2.BOWImgDescriptorExtractor(extract, flann)

def extract_sift(fn):
  im = cv2.imread(fn,0)
  return extract.compute(im, detect.detect(im))[1]

for i in range(8):
  bow_kmeans_trainer.add(extract_sift(path(pos,i)))
  bow_kmeans_trainer.add(extract_sift(path(neg,i)))

voc = bow_kmeans_trainer.cluster()
extract_bow.setVocabulary( voc )

def bow_features(fn):
  im = cv2.imread(fn,0)
  return extract_bow.compute(im, detect.detect(im))

traindata, trainlabels = [],[]
for i in range(20):
  traindata.extend(bow_features(path(pos, i)));
    trainlabels.append(1)
  traindata.extend(bow_features(path(neg, i)));
    trainlabels.append(-1)

svm = cv2.ml.SVM_create()
svm.train(np.array(traindata), cv2.ml.ROW_SAMPLE,
  np.array(trainlabels))

def predict(fn):
  f = bow_features(fn);
  p = svm.predict(f)
  print fn, "\t", p[1][0][0]
  return p

car, notcar = "/home/d3athmast3r/dev/python/study/images/car.jpg",
  "/home/d3athmast3r/dev/python/study/images/bb.jpg"
car_img = cv2.imread(car)
notcar_img = cv2.imread(notcar)
```

```
car_predict = predict(car)
not_car_predict = predict(notcar)

font = cv2.FONT_HERSHEY_SIMPLEX

if (car_predict[1][0][0] == 1.0):
  cv2.putText(car_img,'Car Detected',(10,30), font,
    1,(0,255,0),2,cv2.LINE_AA)

if (not_car_predict[1][0][0] == -1.0):
  cv2.putText(notcar_img,'Car Not Detected',(10,30), font, 1,(0,0,
    255),2,cv2.LINE_AA)

cv2.imshow('BOW + SVM Success', car_img)
cv2.imshow('BOW + SVM Failure', notcar_img)
cv2.waitKey(0)
cv2.destroyAllWindows()
```

What did we just do?

This is quite a lot to assimilate, so let's go through what we've done:

1. First of all, our usual imports are followed by the declaration of the base path of our training images. This will come in handy to avoid rewriting the base path every time we process an image in a particular folder on our computer.

2. After this, we declare a function, path:

    ```
    def path(cls,i):
        return "%s/%s%d.pgm"  % (datapath,cls,i+1)

    pos, neg = "pos-", "neg-"
    ```

More on the path function

This function is a utility method: given the name of a class (in our case, we have two classes, pos and neg) and a numerical index, we return the full path to a particular testing image. Our car dataset contains images named in the following way: pos-x.pgm and neg-x.pgm, where x is a number.

Immediately, you will find the usefulness of this function when iterating through a range of numbers (say, 20), which will allow you to load all images from pos-0.pgm to pos-20.pgm, and the same goes for the negative class.

3. Next up, we'll create two SIFT instances: one to extract keypoints, the other to extract features:

```
detect = cv2.xfeatures2d.SIFT_create()
extract = cv2.xfeatures2d.SIFT_create()
```

4. Whenever you see SIFT involved, you can be pretty sure some feature matching algorithm will be involved too. In our case, we'll create an instance for a FLANN matcher:

```
flann_params = dict(algorithm = 1, trees = 5)flann =
    cv2.FlannBasedMatcher(flann_params, {})
```

> Note that currently, the enum values for FLANN are missing from the Python version of OpenCV 3, so, number 1, which is passed as the algorithm parameter, represents the FLANN_INDEX_KDTREE algorithm. I suspect the final version will be cv2.FLANN_INDEX_ KDTREE, which is a little more helpful. Make sure to check the enum values for the correct flags.

5. Next, we mention the BOW trainer:

```
bow_kmeans_trainer = cv2.BOWKMeansTrainer(40)
```

6. This BOW trainer utilizes 40 clusters. After this, we'll initialize the BOW extractor. This is the BOW class that will be fed a vocabulary of visual words and will try to detect them in the test image:

```
extract_bow = cv2.BOWImgDescriptorExtractor(extract, flann)
```

7. To extract the SIFT features from an image, we build a utility method, which takes the path to the image, reads it in grayscale, and returns the descriptor:

```
def extract_sift(fn):
  im = cv2.imread(fn,0)
  return extract.compute(im, detect.detect(im))[1]
```

At this stage, we have everything we need to start training the BOW trainer.

1. Let's read eight images per class (eight positives and eight negatives) from our dataset:

```
for i in range(8):
  bow_kmeans_trainer.add(extract_sift(path(pos,i)))
  bow_kmeans_trainer.add(extract_sift(path(neg,i)))
```

2. To create the vocabulary of visual words, we'll call the `cluster()` method on the trainer, which performs the k-means classification and returns the said vocabulary. We'll assign this vocabulary to `BOWImgDescriptorExtractor` so that it can extract descriptors from test images:

```
vocabulary = bow_kmeans_trainer.cluster()
extract_bow.setVocabulary(vocabulary)
```

3. In line with other utility functions declared in this script, we'll declare a function that takes the path to an image and returns the descriptor as computed by the BOW descriptor extractor:

```
def bow_features(fn):
    im = cv2.imread(fn,0)
    return extract_bow.compute(im, detect.detect(im))
```

4. Let's create two arrays to accommodate the train data and labels, and populate them with the descriptors generated by `BOWImgDescriptorExtractor`, associating labels to the positive and negative images we're feeding (1 stands for a positive match, -1 for a negative):

```
traindata, trainlabels = [],[]
for i in range(20):
    traindata.extend(bow_features(path(pos, i)));
        trainlabels.append(1)
    traindata.extend(bow_features(path(neg, i)));
        trainlabels.append(-1)
```

5. Now, let's create an instance of an SVM:

```
svm = cv2.ml.SVM_create()
```

6. Then, train it by wrapping the train data and labels into the NumPy arrays:

```
svm.train(np.array(traindata), cv2.ml.ROW_SAMPLE,
    np.array(trainlabels))
```

We're all set with a trained SVM; all that is left to do is to feed the SVM a couple of sample images and see how it behaves.

1. Let's first define another utility method to print the result of our `predict` method and return it:

```
def predict(fn):
    f = bow_features(fn);
    p = svm.predict(f)
    print fn, "\t", p[1][0][0]
    return p
```

2. Let's define two sample image paths and read them as the NumPy arrays:

```
car, notcar =
  "/home/d3athmast3r/dev/python/study/images/car.jpg",
    "/home/d3athmast3r/dev/python/study/images/bb.jpg"
car_img = cv2.imread(car)
notcar_img = cv2.imread(notcar)
```

3. We'll pass these images to the trained SVM, and get the result of the prediction:

```
car_predict = predict(car)
not_car_predict = predict(notcar)
```

Naturally, we're hoping that the car image will be detected as a car (result of `predict()` should be `1.0`), and that the other image will not (result should be `-1.0`), so we will only add text to the images if the result is the expected one.

4. At last, we'll present the images on the screen, hoping to see the correct caption on each:

```
font = cv2.FONT_HERSHEY_SIMPLEX

if (car_predict[1][0][0] == 1.0):
  cv2.putText(car_img,'Car Detected',(10,30), font,
    1,(0,255,0),2,cv2.LINE_AA)

if (not_car_predict[1][0][0] == -1.0):
  cv2.putText(notcar_img,'Car Not Detected',(10,30), font,
    1,(0,0, 255),2,cv2.LINE_AA)

cv2.imshow('BOW + SVM Success', car_img)
cv2.imshow('BOW + SVM Failure', notcar_img)
cv2.waitKey(0)
cv2.destroyAllWindows()
```

The preceding operation produces the following result:

It also results in this:

SVM and sliding windows

Having detected an object is an impressive achievement, but now we want to push this to the next level in these ways:

- Detecting multiple objects of the same kind in an image
- Determining the position of a detected object in an image

To accomplish this, we will use the sliding windows approach. If it's not already clear from the previous explanation of the concept of sliding windows, the rationale behind the adoption of this approach will become more apparent if we take a look at a diagram:

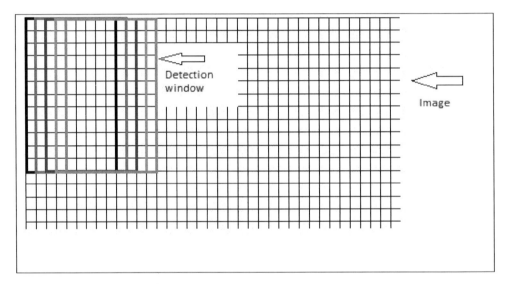

Observe the movement of the block:

1. We take a region of the image, classify it, and then move a predefined step size to the right-hand side. When we reach the rightmost end of the image, we'll reset the x coordinate to 0 and move down a step, and repeat the entire process.
2. At each step, we'll perform a classification with the SVM that was trained with BOW.
3. Keep a track of all the blocks that have *passed* the SVM predict test.
4. When you've finished classifying the entire image, scale the image down and repeat the entire sliding windows process.

Continue rescaling and classifying until you get to a minimum size.

This gives you the chance to detect objects in several regions of the image and at different scales.

At this stage, you will have collected important information about the content of the image; however, there's a problem: it's most likely that you will end up with a number of overlapping blocks that give you a positive score. This means that your image may contain one object that gets detected four or five times, and if you were to report the result of the detection, your report would be quite inaccurate, so here's where non-maximum suppression comes into play.

Example – car detection in a scene

We are now ready to apply all the concepts we learned so far to a real-life example, and create a car detector application that scans an image and draws rectangles around cars.

Let's summarize the process before diving into the code:

1. Obtain a train dataset.
2. Create a BOW trainer and create a visual vocabulary.
3. Train an SVM with the vocabulary.
4. Attempt detection using sliding windows on an image pyramid of a test image.
5. Apply non-maximum suppression to overlapping boxes.
6. Output the result.

Let's also take a look at the structure of the project, as it is a bit more complex than the classic standalone script approach we've adopted until now.

The project structure is as follows:

```
├── car_detector
│   ├── detector.py
│   ├── __init__.py
│   ├── non_maximum.py
│   ├── pyramid.py
│   └── sliding_w112661222.indow.py
└── car_sliding_windows.py
```

The main program is in `car_sliding_windows.py`, and all the utilities are contained in the `car_detector` folder. As we're using Python 2.7, we'll need an `__init__.py` file in the folder for it to be detected as a module.

The four files in the `car_detector` module are as follows:

- The SVM training model
- The non-maximum suppression function
- The image pyramid
- The sliding windows function

Let's examine them one by one, starting from the image pyramid:

```
import cv2

def resize(img, scaleFactor):
  return cv2.resize(img, (int(img.shape[1] * (1 / scaleFactor)),
    int(img.shape[0] * (1 / scaleFactor))),
      interpolation=cv2.INTER_AREA)

def pyramid(image, scale=1.5, minSize=(200, 80)):
  yield image

  while True:
    image = resize(image, scale)
    if image.shape[0] < minSize[1] or image.shape[1] < minSize[0]:
      break

    yield image
```

This module contains two function definitions:

- Resize takes an image and resizes it by a specified factor
- Pyramid takes an image and returns a resized version of it until the minimum constraints of width and height are reached

You will notice that the image is not returned with the `return` keyword but with the `yield` keyword. This is because this function is a so-called generator. If you are not familiar with generators, take a look at https://wiki.python.org/moin/Generators.

This will allow us to obtain a resized image to process in our main program.

Next up is the sliding windows function:

```
def sliding_window(image, stepSize, windowSize):
    for y in xrange(0, image.shape[0], stepSize):
        for x in xrange(0, image.shape[1], stepSize):
            yield (x, y, image[y:y + windowSize[1], x:x +
                windowSize[0]])
```

Again, this is a generator. Although a bit deep-nested, this mechanism is very simple: given an image, return a window that moves of an arbitrary sized step from the left margin towards the right, until the entire width of the image is covered, then goes back to the left margin but down a step, covering the width of the image repeatedly until the bottom right corner of the image is reached. You can visualize this as the same pattern used for writing on a piece of paper: start from the left margin and reach the right margin, then move onto the next line from the left margin.

The last utility is non-maximum suppression, which looks like this (Malisiewicz/Rosebrock's code):

```
def non_max_suppression_fast(boxes, overlapThresh):

    # if there are no boxes, return an empty list

    if len(boxes) == 0:

        return []



    # if the bounding boxes integers, convert them to floats --

    # this is important since we'll be doing a bunch of divisions

    if boxes.dtype.kind == "i":

        boxes = boxes.astype("float")



    # initialize the list of picked indexes

    pick = []
```

```python
# grab the coordinates of the bounding boxes

x1 = boxes[:,0]

y1 = boxes[:,1]

x2 = boxes[:,2]

y2 = boxes[:,3]

scores = boxes[:,4]

# compute the area of the bounding boxes and sort the bounding

# boxes by the score/probability of the bounding box

area = (x2 - x1 + 1) * (y2 - y1 + 1)

idxs = np.argsort(scores)[::-1]


# keep looping while some indexes still remain in the indexes

# list

while len(idxs) > 0:

    # grab the last index in the indexes list and add the

    # index value to the list of picked indexes

    last = len(idxs) - 1

    i = idxs[last]

    pick.append(i)


    # find the largest (x, y) coordinates for the start of

    # the bounding box and the smallest (x, y) coordinates
```

```
# for the end of the bounding box

xx1 = np.maximum(x1[i], x1[idxs[:last]])

yy1 = np.maximum(y1[i], y1[idxs[:last]])

xx2 = np.minimum(x2[i], x2[idxs[:last]])

yy2 = np.minimum(y2[i], y2[idxs[:last]])



# compute the width and height of the bounding box

w = np.maximum(0, xx2 - xx1 + 1)

h = np.maximum(0, yy2 - yy1 + 1)



# compute the ratio of overlap

overlap = (w * h) / area[idxs[:last]]



# delete all indexes from the index list that have

idxs = np.delete(idxs, np.concatenate(([last],

    np.where(overlap > overlapThresh)[0])))



# return only the bounding boxes that were picked using the

# integer data type

return boxes[pick].astype("int")
```

This function simply takes a list of rectangles and sorts them by their score. Starting from the box with the highest score, it eliminates all boxes that overlap beyond a certain threshold by calculating the area of intersection and determining whether it is greater than a certain threshold.

Examining detector.py

Now, let's examine the heart of this program, which is `detector.py`. This a bit long and complex; however, everything should appear much clearer given our newfound familiarity with the concepts of BOW, SVM, and feature detection/extraction.

Here's the code:

```
import cv2
import numpy as np

datapath = "/path/to/CarData/TrainImages/"
SAMPLES = 400

def path(cls,i):
    return "%s/%s%d.pgm"  % (datapath,cls,i+1)

def get_flann_matcher():
  flann_params = dict(algorithm = 1, trees = 5)
  return cv2.FlannBasedMatcher(flann_params, {})

def get_bow_extractor(extract, flann):
  return cv2.BOWImgDescriptorExtractor(extract, flann)

def get_extract_detect():
  return cv2.xfeatures2d.SIFT_create(),
    cv2.xfeatures2d.SIFT_create()

def extract_sift(fn, extractor, detector):
  im = cv2.imread(fn,0)
  return extractor.compute(im, detector.detect(im))[1]

def bow_features(img, extractor_bow, detector):
  return extractor_bow.compute(img, detector.detect(img))

def car_detector():
  pos, neg = "pos-", "neg-"
  detect, extract = get_extract_detect()
  matcher = get_flann_matcher()
  print "building BOWKMeansTrainer..."
  bow_kmeans_trainer = cv2.BOWKMeansTrainer(1000)
  extract_bow = cv2.BOWImgDescriptorExtractor(extract, flann)

  print "adding features to trainer"
  for i in range(SAMPLES):
```

```
    print i
    bow_kmeans_trainer.add(extract_sift(path(pos,i), extract,
      detect))
    bow_kmeans_trainer.add(extract_sift(path(neg,i), extract,
      detect))

  voc = bow_kmeans_trainer.cluster()
  extract_bow.setVocabulary( voc )

  traindata, trainlabels = [],[]
  print "adding to train data"
  for i in range(SAMPLES):
    print i
    traindata.extend(bow_features(cv2.imread(path(pos, i), 0),
      extract_bow, detect))
    trainlabels.append(1)
    traindata.extend(bow_features(cv2.imread(path(neg, i), 0),
      extract_bow, detect))
    trainlabels.append(-1)

  svm = cv2.ml.SVM_create()
  svm.setType(cv2.ml.SVM_C_SVC)
  svm.setGamma(0.5)
  svm.setC(30)
  svm.setKernel(cv2.ml.SVM_RBF)

  svm.train(np.array(traindata), cv2.ml.ROW_SAMPLE,
    np.array(trainlabels))
  return svm, extract_bow
```

Let's go through it. First, we'll import our usual modules, and then set a path for the training images.

Then, we'll define a number of utility functions:

```
def path(cls,i):
    return "%s/%s%d.pgm"  % (datapath,cls,i+1)
```

This function returns the path to an image given a base path and a class name. In our example, we're going to use the `neg-` and `pos-` class names, because this is what the training images are called (that is, `neg-1.pgm`). The last argument is an integer used to compose the final part of the image path.

Next, we'll define a utility function to obtain a FLANN matcher:

```
def get_flann_matcher():
    flann_params = dict(algorithm = 1, trees = 5)
    return cv2.FlannBasedMatcher(flann_params, {})
```

Again, it's not that the integer, 1, passed as an algorithm argument represents `FLANN_INDEX_KDTREE`.

The next two functions return the SIFT feature detectors/extractors and a BOW trainer:

```
def get_bow_extractor(extract, flann):
    return cv2.BOWImgDescriptorExtractor(extract, flann)

def get_extract_detect():
    return cv2.xfeatures2d.SIFT_create(),
        cv2.xfeatures2d.SIFT_create()
```

The next utility is a function used to return features from an image:

```
def extract_sift(fn, extractor, detector):
    im = cv2.imread(fn,0)
    return extractor.compute(im, detector.detect(im))[1]
```

 A SIFT detector detects features, while a SIFT extractor extracts and returns them.

We'll also define a similar utility function to extract the BOW features:

```
def bow_features(img, extractor_bow, detector):
    return extractor_bow.compute(img, detector.detect(img))
```

In the main `car_detector` function, we'll first create the necessary object used to perform feature detection and extraction:

```
    pos, neg = "pos-", "neg-"
    detect, extract = get_extract_detect()
    matcher = get_flann_matcher()
    bow_kmeans_trainer = cv2.BOWKMeansTrainer(1000)
    extract_bow = cv2.BOWImgDescriptorExtractor(extract, flann)
```

Then, we'll add features taken from training images to the trainer:

```
print "adding features to trainer"
for i in range(SAMPLES):
  print i
  bow_kmeans_trainer.add(extract_sift(path(pos,i), extract,
    detect))
```

For each class, we'll add a positive image to the trainer and a negative image.

After this, we'll instruct the trainer to cluster the data into *k* groups.

The clustered data is now our vocabulary of visual words, and we can set the `BOWImgDescriptorExtractor` class' vocabulary in this way:

```
vocabulary = bow_kmeans_trainer.cluster()
  extract_bow.setVocabulary(vocabulary)
```

Associating training data with classes

With a visual vocabulary ready, we can now associate train data with classes. In our case, we have two classes: `-1` for negative results and `1` for positive ones.

Let's populate two arrays, `traindata` and `trainlabels`, containing extracted features and their corresponding labels. Iterating through the dataset, we can quickly set this up with the following code:

```
traindata, trainlabels = [], []
  print "adding to train data"
  for i in range(SAMPLES):
    print i
    traindata.extend(bow_features(cv2.imread(path(pos, i), 0),
      extract_bow, detect))
    trainlabels.append(1)
    traindata.extend(bow_features(cv2.imread(path(neg, i), 0),
      extract_bow, detect))
    trainlabels.append(-1)
```

You will notice that at each cycle, we'll add one positive and one negative image, and then populate the labels with a `1` and a `-1` value to keep the data synchronized with the labels.

Should you wish to train more classes, you could do that by following this pattern:

```
traindata, trainlabels = [], []
print "adding to train data"
for i in range(SAMPLES):
  print i
  traindata.extend(bow_features(cv2.imread(path(class1, i), 0),
    extract_bow, detect))
  trainlabels.append(1)
  traindata.extend(bow_features(cv2.imread(path(class2, i), 0),
    extract_bow, detect))
  trainlabels.append(2)
  traindata.extend(bow_features(cv2.imread(path(class3, i), 0),
    extract_bow, detect))
  trainlabels.append(3)
```

For example, you could train a detector to detect cars and people and perform detection on these in an image containing both cars and people.

Lastly, we'll train the SVM with the following code:

```
svm = cv2.ml.SVM_create()
svm.setType(cv2.ml.SVM_C_SVC)
svm.setGamma(0.5)
svm.setC(30)
svm.setKernel(cv2.ml.SVM_RBF)

svm.train(np.array(traindata), cv2.ml.ROW_SAMPLE,
  np.array(trainlabels))
return svm, extract_bow
```

There are two parameters in particular that I'd like to focus your attention on:

- **C**: With this parameter, you could conceptualize the strictness or severity of the classifier. The higher the value, the less chances of misclassification, but the trade-off is that some positive results may not be detected. On the other hand, a low value may over-fit, so you risk getting false positives.

- **Kernel**: This parameter determines the nature of the classifier: SVM_LINEAR indicates a linear *hyperplane*, which, in practical terms, works very well for a binary classification (the test sample either belongs to a class or it doesn't), while SVM_RBF (**radial basis function**) separates data using the Gaussian functions, which means that the data is split into several kernels defined by these functions. When training the SVM to classify for more than two classes, you will have to use RBF.

Finally, we'll pass the `traindata` and `trainlabels` arrays into the SVM `train` method, and return the SVM and BOW extractor object. This is because in our applications, we don't want to have to recreate the vocabulary every time, so we expose it for reuse.

Dude, where's my car?

We are ready to test our car detector!

Let's first create a simple program that loads an image, and then operates detection using the sliding windows and image pyramid techniques, respectively:

```
import cv2
import numpy as np
from car_detector.detector import car_detector, bow_features
from car_detector.pyramid import pyramid
from car_detector.non_maximum import non_max_suppression_fast as
    nms
from car_detector.sliding_window import sliding_window

def in_range(number, test, thresh=0.2):
  return abs(number - test) < thresh

test_image = "/path/to/cars.jpg"

svm, extractor = car_detector()
detect = cv2.xfeatures2d.SIFT_create()

w, h = 100, 40
img = cv2.imread(test_img)

rectangles = []
counter = 1
scaleFactor = 1.25
scale = 1
font = cv2.FONT_HERSHEY_PLAIN

for resized in pyramid(img, scaleFactor):
  scale = float(img.shape[1]) / float(resized.shape[1])
  for (x, y, roi) in sliding_window(resized, 20, (w, h)):

    if roi.shape[1] != w or roi.shape[0] != h:
      continue

    try:
```

```
        bf = bow_features(roi, extractor, detect)
        _, result = svm.predict(bf)
        a, res = svm.predict(bf, flags=cv2.ml.STAT_MODEL_RAW_OUTPUT)
        print "Class: %d, Score: %f" % (result[0][0], res[0][0])
        score = res[0][0]
        if result[0][0] == 1:
          if score < -1.0:
            rx, ry, rx2, ry2 = int(x * scale), int(y * scale),
              int((x+w) * scale), int((y+h) * scale)
            rectangles.append([rx, ry, rx2, ry2, abs(score)])
      except:
        pass

      counter += 1

  windows = np.array(rectangles)
  boxes = nms(windows, 0.25)


  for (x, y, x2, y2, score) in boxes:
    print x, y, x2, y2, score
    cv2.rectangle(img, (int(x),int(y)), (int(x2), int(y2)),(0, 255,
      0), 1)
    cv2.putText(img, "%f" % score, (int(x),int(y)), font, 1, (0,
      255, 0))

  cv2.imshow("img", img)
  cv2.waitKey(0)
```

The notable part of the program is the function within the pyramid/sliding window loop:

```
        bf = bow_features(roi, extractor, detect)
        _, result = svm.predict(bf)
        a, res = svm.predict(bf, flags=cv2.ml.STAT_MODEL_RAW_OUTPUT)
        print "Class: %d, Score: %f" % (result[0][0], res[0][0])
        score = res[0][0]
        if result[0][0] == 1:
          if score < -1.0:
            rx, ry, rx2, ry2 = int(x * scale), int(y * scale),
              int((x+w) * scale), int((y+h) * scale)
            rectangles.append([rx, ry, rx2, ry2, abs(score)])
```

Here, we extract the features of the **region of interest** (**ROI**), which corresponds to the current sliding window, and then we call `predict` on the extracted features. The `predict` method has an optional parameter, `flags`, which returns the score of the prediction (contained at the `[0][0]` value).

 A word on the score of the prediction: the lower the value, the higher the confidence that the classified element really belongs to the class.

So, we'll set an arbitrary threshold of `-1.0` for classified windows, and all windows with less than `-1.0` are going to be taken as good results. As you experiment with your SVMs, you may tweak this to your liking until you find a golden mean that assures best results.

Finally, we add the computed coordinates of the sliding window (meaning, we multiply the current coordinates by the scale of the current layer in the image pyramid so that it gets correctly represented in the final drawing) to the array of rectangles.

There's one last operation we need to perform before drawing our final result: non-maximum suppression.

We turn the rectangles array into a NumPy array (to allow certain kind of operations that are only possible with NumPy), and then apply NMS:

```
windows = np.array(rectangles)
boxes = nms(windows, 0.25)
```

Finally, we proceed with displaying all our results; for the sake of convenience, I've also printed the score obtained for all the remaining windows:

This is a remarkably accurate result!

A final note on SVM: you don't need to train a detector every time you want to use it, which would be extremely impractical. You can use the following code:

```
svm.save('/path/to/serialized/svmxml')
```

You can subsequently reload it with a load method and feed it test images or frames.

Summary

In this chapter, we talked about numerous object detection concepts, such as HOG, BOW, SVM, and some useful techniques, such as image pyramid, sliding windows, and non-maximum suppression.

We introduced the concept of machine learning and explored the various approaches used to train a custom detector, including how to create or obtain a training dataset and classify data. Finally, we put this knowledge to good use by creating a car detector from scratch and verifying its correct functioning.

All these concepts form the foundation of the next chapter, in which we will utilize object detection and classification techniques in the context of making videos, and learn how to track objects to retain information that can potentially be used for business or application purposes.

8
Tracking Objects

In this chapter, we will explore the vast topic of object tracking, which is the process of locating a moving object in a movie or video feed from a camera. Real-time object tracking is a critical task in many computer vision applications such as surveillance, perceptual user interfaces, augmented reality, object-based video compression, and driver assistance.

Tracking objects can be accomplished in several ways, with the optimal technique being largely dependent on the task at hand. We will learn how to identify moving objects and track them across frames.

Detecting moving objects

The first task that needs to be accomplished for us to be able to track anything in a video is to identify those regions of a video frame that correspond to moving objects.

There are many ways to track objects in a video, all of them fulfilling a slightly different purpose. For example, you may want to track anything that moves, in which case differences between frames are going to be of help; you may want to track a hand moving in a video, in which case Meanshift based on the color of the skin is the most appropriate solution; you may want to track a particular object of which you know the aspect, in which case techniques such as template matching will be of help.

Object tracking techniques can get quite complex, let's explore them in the ascending order of difficulty, starting from the simplest technique.

Basic motion detection

The first and most intuitive solution is to calculate the differences between frames, or between a frame considered "background" and all the other frames.

Let's look at an example of this approach:

```
import cv2
import numpy as np

camera = cv2.VideoCapture(0)

es = cv2.getStructuringElement(cv2.MORPH_ELLIPSE, (9,4))
kernel = np.ones((5,5),np.uint8)
background = None

while (True):
  ret, frame = camera.read()
  if background is None:
    background = cv2.cvtColor(frame, cv2.COLOR_BGR2GRAY)
    background = cv2.GaussianBlur(background, (21, 21), 0)
    continue

  gray_frame = cv2.cvtColor(frame, cv2.COLOR_BGR2GRAY)
  gray_frame = cv2.GaussianBlur(gray_frame, (21, 21), 0)

  diff = cv2.absdiff(background, gray_frame)
  diff = cv2.threshold(diff, 25, 255, cv2.THRESH_BINARY)[1]
  diff = cv2.dilate(diff, es, iterations = 2)
  image, cnts, hierarchy = cv2.findContours(diff.copy(),
    cv2.RETR_EXTERNAL, cv2.CHAIN_APPROX_SIMPLE)

  for c in cnts:
    if cv2.contourArea(c) < 1500:
      continue
    (x, y, w, h) = cv2.boundingRect(c)
    cv2.rectangle(frame, (x, y), (x + w, y + h), (0, 255, 0), 2)

  cv2.imshow("contours", frame)
  cv2.imshow("dif", diff)
  if cv2.waitKey(1000 / 12) & 0xff == ord("q"):
    break

cv2.destroyAllWindows()
camera.release()
```

After the necessary imports, we open the video feed obtained from the default system camera, and we set the first frame as the background of the entire feed. Each frame read from that point onward is processed to calculate the difference between the background and the frame itself. This is a trivial operation:

```
diff = cv2.threshold(diff, 25, 255, cv2.THRESH_BINARY)[1]
```

Before we get to do that, though, we need to prepare our frame for processing. The first thing we do is convert the frame to grayscale and blur it a bit:

```
gray_frame = cv2.cvtColor(frame, cv2.COLOR_BGR2GRAY)
gray_frame = cv2.GaussianBlur(gray_frame, (21, 21), 0)
```

 You may wonder about the blurring: the reason why we blur the image is that, in each video feed, there's a natural noise coming from natural vibrations, changes in lighting, and the noise generated by the camera itself. We want to smooth this noise out so that it doesn't get detected as motion and consequently get tracked.

Now that our frame is grayscaled and smoothed, we can calculate the difference compared to the background (which has also been grayscaled and smoothed), and obtain a map of differences. This is not the only processing step, though. We're also going to apply a threshold, so as to obtain a black and white image, and dilate the image so holes and imperfections get normalized, like so:

```
diff = cv2.absdiff(background, gray_frame)
diff = cv2.threshold(diff, 25, 255, cv2.THRESH_BINARY)[1]
diff = cv2.dilate(diff, es, iterations = 2)
```

Note that eroding and dilating can also act as a noise filter, much like the blurring we applied, and that it can also be obtained in one function call using `cv2.morphologyEx`, we show both steps explicitly for transparency purposes. All that is left to do at this point is to find the contours of all the white blobs in the calculated difference map, and display them. Optionally, we only display contours for rectangles greater than an arbitrary threshold, so tiny movements are not displayed. Naturally, this is up to you and your application needs. With a constant lighting and a very noiseless camera, you may wish to have no threshold on the minimum size of the contours. This is how we display the rectangles:

```
image, cnts, hierarchy = cv2.findContours(diff.copy(),
    cv2.RETR_EXTERNAL, cv2.CHAIN_APPROX_SIMPLE)
for c in cnts:
    if cv2.contourArea(c) < 1500:
        continue
    (x, y, w, h) = cv2.boundingRect(c)
```

```
        cv2.rectangle(frame, (x, y), (x + w, y + h), (255, 255, 0), 2)

    cv2.imshow("contours", frame)
    cv2.imshow("dif", diff)
```

OpenCV offers two very handy functions:

- `cv2.findContours`: This function computes the contours of subjects in an image
- `cv2.boundinRect`: This function calculates their bounding box

So there you have it, a basic motion detector with rectangles around subjects. The final result is something like this:

For such a simple technique, this is quite accurate. However, there are a few drawbacks that make this approach unsuitable for all business needs, most notably the fact that you need a first "default" frame to set as a background. In situations such as—for example—outdoor cameras, with lights changing quite constantly, this process results in a quite inflexible approach, so we need a bit more intelligence into our system. That's where background subtractors come into play.

Background subtractors – KNN, MOG2, and GMG

OpenCV provides a class called `BackgroundSubtractor`, which is a handy way to operate foreground and background segmentation.

This works similarly to the GrabCut algorithm we analyzed in *Chapter 3*, *Processing Images with OpenCV 3*, however, `BackgroundSubtractor` is a fully fledged class with a plethora of methods that not only perform background subtraction, but also improve background detection in time through machine learning and lets you save the classifier to a file.

To familiarize ourselves with `BackgroundSubtractor`, let's look at a basic example:

```python
import numpy as np
import cv2

cap = cv2.VideoCapture')

mog = cv2.createBackgroundSubtractorMOG2()

while(1):
    ret, frame = cap.read()
    fgmask = mog.apply(frame)
    cv2.imshow('frame',fgmask)
    if cv2.waitKey(30) & 0xff:
        break

cap.release()
cv2.destroyAllWindows()
```

Let's go through this in order. First of all, let's talk about the background subtractor object. There are three background subtractors available in OpenCV 3: **K-Nearest Neighbors (KNN)**, **Mixture of Gaussians (MOG2)**, and **Geometric Multigrid (GMG)**, corresponding to the algorithm used to compute the background subtraction.

You may remember that we already elaborated on the topic of foreground and background detection in *Chapter 5, Depth Estimation and Segmentation*, in particular when we talked about GrabCut and Watershed.

So why do we need the `BackgroundSubtractor` classes? The main reason behind this is that `BackgroundSubtractor` classes are specifically built with video analysis in mind, which means that the OpenCV `BackgroundSubtractor` classes "learn" something about the environment with every frame. For example, with GMG, you can specify the number of frames used to initialize the video analysis, with the default being 120 (roughly 5 seconds with average cameras). The constant aspect about the `BackgroundSubtractor` classes is that they operate a comparison between frames and they store a history, which allows them to improve motion analysis results as time passes.

Another fundamental (and frankly, quite amazing) feature of the `BackgroundSubtractor` classes is the ability to compute shadows. This is absolutely vital for an accurate reading of video frames; by detecting shadows, you can exclude shadow areas (by thresholding them) from the objects you detected, and concentrate on the real features. It also greatly reduces the unwanted "merging" of objects. An image comparison will give you a good idea of the concept I'm trying to illustrate. Here's a sample of background subtraction without shadow detection:

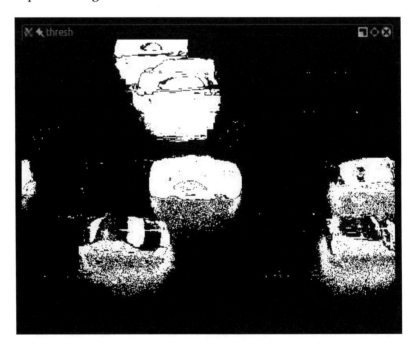

Here's an example of shadow detection (with shadows thresholded):

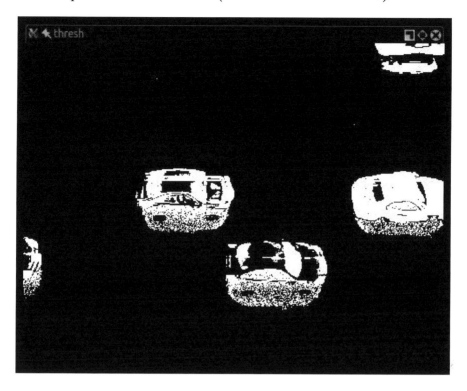

Note that shadow detection isn't absolutely perfect, but it helps bring the object contours back to the object's original shape. Let's take a look at a reimplemented example of motion detection utilizing BackgroundSubtractorKNN:

```
import cv2
import numpy as np

bs = cv2.createBackgroundSubtractorKNN(detectShadows = True)
camera = cv2.VideoCapture("/path/to/movie.flv")

while True:
  ret, frame = camera.read()
  fgmask = bs.apply(frame)
  th = cv2.threshold(fgmask.copy(), 244, 255,
    cv2.THRESH_BINARY)[1]
  dilated = cv2.dilate(th,
    cv2.getStructuringElement(cv2.MORPH_ELLIPSE, (3,3)),
      iterations = 2)
```

```
image, contours, hier = cv2.findContours(dilated,
  cv2.RETR_EXTERNAL, cv2.CHAIN_APPROX_SIMPLE)
for c in contours:
  if cv2.contourArea(c) > 1600:
    (x,y,w,h) = cv2.boundingRect(c)
    cv2.rectangle(frame, (x,y), (x+w, y+h), (255, 255, 0), 2)

cv2.imshow("mog", fgmask)
cv2.imshow("thresh", th)
cv2.imshow("detection", frame)
if cv2.waitKey(30) & 0xff == 27:
    break

camera.release()
cv2.destroyAllWindows()
```

As a result of the accuracy of the subtractor, and its ability to detect shadows, we obtain a really precise motion detection, in which even objects that are next to each other don't get merged into one detection, as shown in the following screenshot:

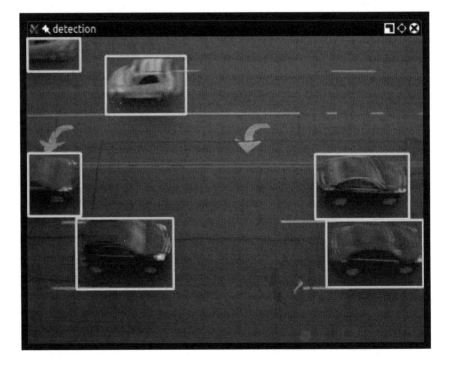

That's a remarkable result for fewer than 30 lines of code!

The core of the entire program is the `apply()` method of the background subtractor; it computes a foreground mask, which can be used as a basis for the rest of the processing:

```
fgmask = bs.apply(frame)
th = cv2.threshold(fgmask.copy(), 244, 255, cv2.THRESH_BINARY)[1]
dilated = cv2.dilate(th,
    cv2.getStructuringElement(cv2.MORPH_ELLIPSE, (3,3)),
        iterations = 2)
image, contours, hier = cv2.findContours(dilated,
    cv2.RETR_EXTERNAL, cv2.CHAIN_APPROX_SIMPLE)
for c in contours:
    if cv2.contourArea(c) > 1600:
        (x,y,w,h) = cv2.boundingRect(c)
        cv2.rectangle(frame, (x,y), (x+w, y+h), (255, 255, 0), 2)
```

Once a foreground mask is obtained, we can apply a threshold: the foreground mask has white values for the foreground and gray for shadows; thus, in the thresholded image, all pixels that are not almost pure white (244-255) are binarized to 0 instead of 1.

From there, we proceed with the same approach we adopted for the basic motion detection example: identifying objects, detecting contours, and drawing them on the original frame.

Meanshift and CAMShift

Background subtraction is a really effective technique, but not the only one available to track objects in a video. Meanshift is an algorithm that tracks objects by finding the maximum density of a discrete sample of a probability function (in our case, a region of interest in an image) and recalculating it at the next frame, which gives the algorithm an indication of the direction in which the object has moved.

This calculation gets repeated until the centroid matches the original one, or remains unaltered even after consecutive iterations of the calculation. This final matching is called **convergence**. For reference, the algorithm was first described in the paper, *The estimation of the gradient of a density function, with applications in pattern recognition, Fukunaga K. and Hoestetler L., IEEE, 1975*, which is available at `http://ieeexplore.ieee.org/xpl/login.jsp?tp=&arnumber=1055330&url=http%3A%2F%2Fieeexplore.ieee.org%2Fxpls%2Fabs_all.jsp%3Farnumber%3D1055330` (note that this paper is not free for download).

Here's a visual representation of this process:

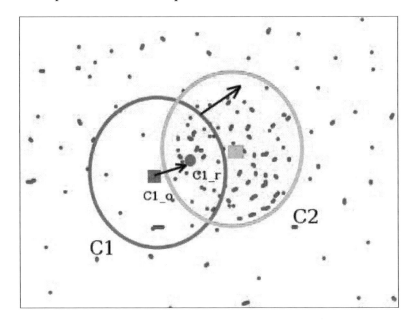

Aside from the theory, Meanshift is very useful when tracking a particular region of interest in a video, and this has a series of implications; for example, if you don't know a priori what the region you want to track is, you're going to have to manage this cleverly and develop programs that dynamically start tracking (and cease tracking) certain areas of the video, depending on arbitrary criteria. One example could be that you operate object detection with a trained SVM, and then start using Meanshift to track a detected object.

Let's not make our life complicated from the very beginning, though; let's first get familiar with Meanshift, and then use it in more complex scenarios.

We will start by simply marking a region of interest and keeping track of it, like so:

```python
import numpy as np
import cv2

cap = cv2.VideoCapture(0)
ret,frame = cap.read()
r,h,c,w = 10, 200, 10, 200
track_window = (c,r,w,h)

roi = frame[r:r+h, c:c+w]
```

```
hsv_roi = cv2.cvtColor(frame, cv2.COLOR_BGR2HSV)
mask = cv2.inRange(hsv_roi, np.array((100., 30.,32.)),
    np.array((180.,120.,255.))))

roi_hist = cv2.calcHist([hsv_roi],[0],mask,[180],[0,180])
cv2.normalize(roi_hist,roi_hist,0,255,cv2.NORM_MINMAX)

term_crit = ( cv2.TERM_CRITERIA_EPS | cv2.TERM_CRITERIA_COUNT, 10,
    1 )

while True:
    ret ,frame = cap.read()

    if ret == True:
        hsv = cv2.cvtColor(frame, cv2.COLOR_BGR2HSV)
        dst = cv2.calcBackProject([hsv],[0],roi_hist,[0,180],1)

        # apply meanshift to get the new location
        ret, track_window = cv2.meanShift(dst, track_window,
            term_crit)

        # Draw it on image
        x,y,w,h = track_window
        img2 = cv2.rectangle(frame, (x,y), (x+w,y+h), 255,2)
        cv2.imshow('img2',img2)

        k = cv2.waitKey(60) & 0xff
        if k == 27:
            break

    else:
        break

cv2.destroyAllWindows()
cap.release()
```

In the preceding code, I supplied the HSV values for tracking some shades of lilac, and here's the result:

If you ran the code on your machine, you'd notice how the Meanshift window actually looks for the specified color range; if it doesn't find it, you'll just see the window wobbling (it actually looks a bit impatient). If an object with the specified color range enters the window, the window will then start tracking it.

Let's examine the code so that we can fully understand how Meanshift performs this tracking operation.

Color histograms

Before showing the code for the preceding example, though, here is a not-so-brief digression on color histograms and the two very important built-in functions of OpenCV: `calcHist` and `calcBackProject`.

The function, `calcHist`, calculates color histograms of an image, so the next logical step is to explain the concept of color histograms. A color histogram is a representation of the color distribution of an image. On the x axis of the representation, we have color values, and on the y axis, we have the number of pixels corresponding to the color values.

Let's look at a visual representation of this concept, hoping the adage, "a picture speaks a thousand words", will apply in this instance too:

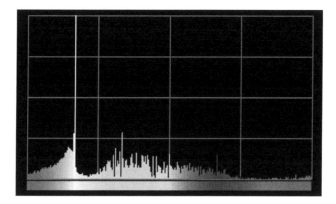

The picture shows a representation of a color histogram with one column per value from 0 to 180 (note that OpenCV uses H values 0-180. Other systems may use 0-360 or 0-255).

Aside from Meanshift, color histograms are used for a number of different and useful image and video processing operations.

The calcHist function

The calcHist() function in OpenCV has the following Python signature:

```
calcHist(...)
     calcHist(images, channels, mask, histSize, ranges[, hist[,
          accumulate]]) -> hist
```

The description of the parameters (as taken from the official OpenCV documentation) are as follows:

Parameter	Description
images	This parameter is the source arrays. They all should have the same depth, CV_8U or CV_32F , and the same size. Each of them can have an arbitrary number of channels.
channels	This parameter is the list of the dims channels used to compute the histogram.
mask	This parameter is the optional mask. If the matrix is not empty, it must be an 8-bit array of the same size as images[i]. The nonzero mask elements mark the array elements counted in the histogram.
histSize	This parameter is the array of histogram sizes in each dimension.

Parameter	Description
ranges	This parameter is the array of the dims arrays of the histogram bin boundaries in each dimension.
hist	This parameter is the output histogram, which is a dense or sparse dims (dimensional) array.
accumulate	This parameter is the accumulation flag. If it is set, the histogram is not cleared in the beginning when it is allocated. This feature enables you to compute a single histogram from several sets of arrays, or to update the histogram in time.

In our example, we calculate the histograms of the region of interest like so:

```
roi_hist = cv2.calcHist([hsv_roi],[0],mask,[180],[0,180])
```

This can be interpreted as the calculation of color histograms for an array of images containing only the region of interest in the HSV space. In this region, we compute only the image values corresponding to the mask values not equal to 0, with 18 histogram columns, and with each histogram having 0 as the lower boundary and 180 as the upper boundary.

This is rather convoluted to describe but, once you have familiarized yourself with the concept of a histogram, the pieces of the puzzle should click into place.

The calcBackProject function

The other function that covers a vital role in the Meanshift algorithm (but not only this) is calcBackProject, which is short for **histogram back projection** (calculation). A histogram back projection is so called because it takes a histogram and projects it back onto an image, with the result being the probability that each pixel will belong to the image that generated the histogram in the first place. Therefore, calcBackProject gives a probability estimation that a certain image is equal or similar to a model image (from which the original histogram was generated).

Again, if you thought calcHist was a bit convoluted, calcBackProject is probably even more complex!

In summary

The calcHist function extracts a color histogram from an image, giving a statistical representation of the colors in an image, and calcBackProject helps in calculating the probability of each pixel of an image belonging to the original image.

Back to the code

Let's get back to our example. First our usual imports, and then we mark the initial region of interest:

```
cap = cv2.VideoCapture(0)
ret,frame = cap.read()
r,h,c,w = 10, 200, 10, 200
track_window = (c,r,w,h)
```

Then, we extract and convert the ROI to HSV color space:

```
roi = frame[r:r+h, c:c+w]
hsv_roi =  cv2.cvtColor(frame, cv2.COLOR_BGR2HSV)
```

Now, we create a mask to include all pixels of the ROI with HSV values between the lower and upper bounds:

```
mask = cv2.inRange(hsv_roi, np.array((100., 30.,32.)),
    np.array((180.,120.,255.)))
```

Next, we calculate the histograms of the ROI:

```
roi_hist = cv2.calcHist([hsv_roi],[0],mask,[180],[0,180])
cv2.normalize(roi_hist,roi_hist,0,255,cv2.NORM_MINMAX)
```

After the histograms are calculated, the values are normalized to be included within the range 0-255.

Meanshift performs a number of iterations before reaching convergence; however, this convergence is not assured. So, OpenCV allows us to pass so-called termination criteria, which is a way to specify the behavior of Meanshift with regard to terminating the series of calculations:

```
term_crit = ( cv2.TERM_CRITERIA_EPS | cv2.TERM_CRITERIA_COUNT, 10,
    1 )
```

In this particular case, we're specifying a behavior that instructs Meanshift to stop calculating the centroid shift after ten iterations or if the centroid has moved at least 1 pixel. That first flag (EPS or CRITERIA_COUNT) indicates we're going to use either of the two criteria (count or "epsilon", meaning the minimum movement).

Now that we have a histogram calculated, and termination criteria for Meanshift, we can start our usual infinite loop, grab the current frame from the camera, and start processing it. The first thing we do is switch to HSV color space:

```
if ret == True:
        hsv = cv2.cvtColor(frame, cv2.COLOR_BGR2HSV)
```

Now that we have an HSV array, we can operate the long awaited histogram back projection:

```
dst = cv2.calcBackProject([hsv],[0],roi_hist,[0,180],1)
```

The result of `calcBackProject` is a matrix. If you printed it to console, it looks more or less like this:

```
[[  0    0    0 ...,   0   0   0]
 [  0    0    0 ...,   0   0   0]
 [  0    0    0 ...,   0   0   0]

 ...,
 [  0    0   20 ...,   0   0   0]
 [ 78   20    0 ...,   0   0   0]
 [255  137   20 ...,   0   0   0]]
```

Each pixel is represented with its probability.

This matrix can the finally be passed into Meanshift, together with the track window and the termination criteria as outlined by the Python signature of `cv2.meanShift`:

```
meanShift(...)
    meanShift(probImage, window, criteria) -> retval, window
```

So here it is:

```
ret, track_window = cv2.meanShift(dst, track_window, term_crit)
```

Finally, we calculate the new coordinates of the window, draw a rectangle to display it in the frame, and then show it:

```
x,y,w,h = track_window
img2 = cv2.rectangle(frame, (x,y), (x+w,y+h), 255,2)
cv2.imshow('img2',img2)
```

That's it. You should by now have a good idea of color histograms, back projections, and Meanshift. However, there remains one issue to be resolved with the preceding program: the size of the window does not change with the size of the object in the frames being tracked.

One of the authorities in computer vision and author of the seminal book, *Learning OpenCV, Gary Bradski, O'Reilly*, published a paper in 1988 to improve the accuracy of Meanshift, and described a new algorithm called **Continuously Adaptive Meanshift (CAMShift)**, which is very similar to Meanshift but also adapts the size of the track window when Meanshift reaches convergence.

CAMShift

While CAMShift adds complexity to Meanshift, the implementation of the
the preceding program using CAMShift is surprisingly (or not?) similar to the
Meanshift example, with the main difference being that, after the call to `CamShift`,
the rectangle is drawn with a particular rotation that follows the rotation of the
object being tracked.

Here's the code reimplemented with CAMShift:

```
import numpy as np
import cv2

cap = cv2.VideoCapture(0)

# take first frame of the video
ret,frame = cap.read()

# setup initial location of window
r,h,c,w = 300,200,400,300  # simply hardcoded the values
track_window = (c,r,w,h)


roi = frame[r:r+h, c:c+w]
hsv_roi =  cv2.cvtColor(frame, cv2.COLOR_BGR2HSV)
mask = cv2.inRange(hsv_roi, np.array((100., 30.,32.)),
    np.array((180.,120.,255.)))
roi_hist = cv2.calcHist([hsv_roi],[0],mask,[180],[0,180])
cv2.normalize(roi_hist,roi_hist,0,255,cv2.NORM_MINMAX)
term_crit = ( cv2.TERM_CRITERIA_EPS | cv2.TERM_CRITERIA_COUNT, 10,
    1 )

while(1):
    ret ,frame = cap.read()

    if ret == True:
        hsv = cv2.cvtColor(frame, cv2.COLOR_BGR2HSV)
        dst = cv2.calcBackProject([hsv],[0],roi_hist,[0,180],1)

        ret, track_window = cv2.CamShift(dst, track_window,
            term_crit)
        pts = cv2.boxPoints(ret)
        pts = np.int0(pts)
```

```
        img2 = cv2.polylines(frame,[pts],True, 255,2)

        cv2.imshow('img2',img2)
        k = cv2.waitKey(60) & 0xff
        if k == 27:
            break

    else:
        break

cv2.destroyAllWindows()
cap.release()
```

The difference between the CAMShift code and the Meanshift one lies in these four lines:

```
ret, track_window = cv2.CamShift(dst, track_window, term_crit)
pts = cv2.boxPoints(ret)
pts = np.int0(pts)
img2 = cv2.polylines(frame,[pts],True, 255,2)
```

The method signature of `CamShift` is identical to Meanshift.

The `boxPoints` function finds the vertices of a rotated rectangle, while the polylines function draws the lines of the rectangle on the frame.

By now, you should be familiar with the three approaches we adopted for tracking objects: basic motion detection, Meanshift, and CAMShift.

Let's now explore another technique: the Kalman filter.

The Kalman filter

The Kalman filter is an algorithm mainly (but not only) developed by Rudolf Kalman in the late 1950s, and has found practical application in many fields, particularly navigation systems for all sorts of vehicles from nuclear submarines to aircrafts.

The Kalman filter operates recursively on streams of noisy input data (which in computer vision is normally a video feed) to produce a statistically optimal estimate of the underlying system state (the position inside the video).

Let's take a quick example to conceptualize the Kalman filter and translate the preceding (purposely broad and generic) definition into plainer English. Think of a small red ball on a table, and imagine you have a camera pointing at the scene. You identify the ball as the subject to be tracked, and flick it with your fingers. The ball will start rolling on the table, following the laws of motion we're familiar with.

If the ball is rolling at a speed of 1 meter per second (1 m/s) in a particular direction, you don't need the Kalman filter to estimate where the ball will be in 1 second's time: it will be 1 meter away. The Kalman filter applies these laws to predict an object's position in the current video frame based on observations gathered in the previous frames. Naturally, the Kalman filter cannot know about a pencil on the table deflecting the course of the ball, but it can adjust for this kind of unforeseeable event.

Predict and update

From the preceding description, we gather that the Kalman filter algorithm is divided into two phases:

- **Predict**: In the first phase, the Kalman filter uses the covariance calculated up to the current point in time to estimate the object's new position
- **Update**: In the second phase, it records the object's position and adjusts the covariance for the next cycle of calculations

This adjustment is—in OpenCV terms—a correction, hence the API of the KalmanFilter class in the Python bindings of OpenCV is as follows:

```
class KalmanFilter(__builtin__.object)
 |   Methods defined here:
 |
 |   __repr__(...)
 |       x.__repr__() <==> repr(x)
 |
 |   correct(...)
 |       correct(measurement) -> retval
 |
 |   predict(...)
 |       predict([, control]) -> retval
```

We can deduce that, in our programs, we will call predict() to estimate the position of an object, and correct() to instruct the Kalman filter to adjust its calculations.

An example

Ultimately, we will aim to use the Kalman filter in combination with CAMShift to obtain the highest degree of accuracy and performance. However, before we go into such levels of complexity, let's analyze a simple example, specifically one that seems to be very common on the Web when it comes to the Kalman filter and OpenCV: mouse tracking.

In the following example, we will draw an empty frame and two lines: one corresponding to the actual movement of the mouse, and the other corresponding to the Kalman filter prediction. Here's the code:

```python
import cv2
import numpy as np

frame = np.zeros((800, 800, 3), np.uint8)
last_measurement = current_measurement = np.array((2,1),
    np.float32)
last_prediction = current_prediction = np.zeros((2,1), np.float32)

def mousemove(event, x, y, s, p):
    global frame, current_measurement, measurements,
        last_measurement, current_prediction, last_prediction
    last_prediction = current_prediction
    last_measurement = current_measurement
    current_measurement =
        np.array([[np.float32(x)],[np.float32(y)]])
    kalman.correct(current_measurement)
    current_prediction = kalman.predict()
    lmx, lmy = last_measurement[0], last_measurement[1]
    cmx, cmy = current_measurement[0], current_measurement[1]
    lpx, lpy = last_prediction[0], last_prediction[1]
    cpx, cpy = current_prediction[0], current_prediction[1]
    cv2.line(frame, (lmx, lmy), (cmx, cmy), (0,100,0))
    cv2.line(frame, (lpx, lpy), (cpx, cpy), (0,0,200))


cv2.namedWindow("kalman_tracker")
cv2.setMouseCallback("kalman_tracker", mousemove)

kalman = cv2.KalmanFilter(4,2)
kalman.measurementMatrix =
    np.array([[1,0,0,0],[0,1,0,0]],np.float32)
kalman.transitionMatrix =
    np.array([[1,0,1,0],[0,1,0,1],[0,0,1,0],[0,0,0,1]],np.float32)
```

```
kalman.processNoiseCov =
    np.array([[1,0,0,0],[0,1,0,0],[0,0,1,0],[0,0,0,1]],np.float32)
        * 0.03

while True:
    cv2.imshow("kalman_tracker", frame)
    if (cv2.waitKey(30) & 0xFF) == 27:
        break

cv2.destroyAllWindows()
```

As usual, let's analyze it step by step. After the packages import, we create an empty frame, of size 800 x 800, and then initialize the arrays that will take the coordinates of the measurements and predictions of the mouse movements:

```
frame = np.zeros((800, 800, 3), np.uint8)
last_measurement = current_measurement = np.array((2,1),
    np.float32)
last_prediction = current_prediction = np.zeros((2,1), np.float32)
```

Then, we declare the mouse move `Callback` function, which is going to handle the drawing of the tracking. The mechanism is quite simple; we store the last measurements and last prediction, correct the Kalman with the current measurement, calculate the Kalman prediction, and finally draw two lines, from the last measurement to the current and from the last prediction to the current:

```
def mousemove(event, x, y, s, p):
    global frame, current_measurement, measurements,
        last_measurement, current_prediction, last_prediction
    last_prediction = current_prediction
    last_measurement = current_measurement
    current_measurement =
        np.array([[np.float32(x)],[np.float32(y)]])
    kalman.correct(current_measurement)
    current_prediction = kalman.predict()
    lmx, lmy = last_measurement[0], last_measurement[1]
    cmx, cmy = current_measurement[0], current_measurement[1]
    lpx, lpy = last_prediction[0], last_prediction[1]
    cpx, cpy = current_prediction[0], current_prediction[1]
    cv2.line(frame, (lmx, lmy), (cmx, cmy), (0,100,0))
    cv2.line(frame, (lpx, lpy), (cpx, cpy), (0,0,200))
```

The next step is to initialize the window and set the `Callback` function. OpenCV handles mouse events with the `setMouseCallback` function; specific events must be handled using the first parameter of the `Callback` (event) function that determines what kind of event has been triggered (click, move, and so on):

```
cv2.namedWindow("kalman_tracker")
cv2.setMouseCallback("kalman_tracker", mousemove)
```

Now we're ready to create the Kalman filter:

```
kalman = cv2.KalmanFilter(4,2)
kalman.measurementMatrix =
    np.array([[1,0,0,0],[0,1,0,0]],np.float32)
kalman.transitionMatrix =
    np.array([[1,0,1,0],[0,1,0,1],[0,0,1,0],[0,0,0,1]],np.float32)
kalman.processNoiseCov =
    np.array([[1,0,0,0],[0,1,0,0],[0,0,1,0],[0,0,0,1]],np.float32)
        * 0.03
```

The Kalman filter class takes optional parameters in its constructor (from the OpenCV documentation):

- `dynamParams`: This parameter states the dimensionality of the state
- `MeasureParams`: This parameter states the dimensionality of the measurement
- `ControlParams`: This parameter states the dimensionality of the control
- `vector.type`: This parameter states the type of the created matrices that should be `CV_32F` or `CV_64F`

I found the preceding parameters (both for the constructor and the Kalman properties) to work very well.

From this point on, the program is straightforward; every mouse movement triggers a Kalman prediction, both the actual position of the mouse and the Kalman prediction are drawn in the frame, which is continuously displayed. If you move your mouse around, you'll notice that, if you make a sudden turn at high speed, the prediction line will have a wider trajectory, which is consistent with the momentum of the mouse movement at the time. Here's a sample result:

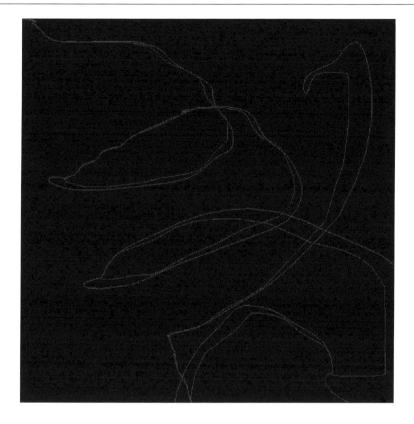

A real-life example – tracking pedestrians

Up to this point, we have familiarized ourselves with the concepts of motion detection, object detection, and object tracking, so I imagine you are anxious to put this newfound knowledge to good use in a real-life scenario. Let's do just that by examining the video feed of a surveillance camera and tracking pedestrians in it.

First of all, we need a sample video; if you download the OpenCV source, you will find the perfect video file for this purpose in `<opencv_dir>/samples/data/768x576.avi`.

Now that we have the perfect asset to analyze, let's start building the application.

The application workflow

The application will adhere to the following logic:

1. Examine the first frame.
2. Examine the following frames and perform background subtraction to identify pedestrians in the scene at the start of the scene.
3. Establish an ROI per pedestrian, and use Kalman/CAMShift to track giving an ID to each pedestrian.
4. Examine the next frames for new pedestrians entering the scene.

If this were a real-world application, you would probably store pedestrian information to obtain information such as the average permanence of a pedestrian in the scene and most likely routes. However, this is all beyond the remit of this example application.

In a real-world application, you would make sure to identify new pedestrians entering the scene, but for now, we'll focus on tracking those objects that are in the scene at the start of the video, utilizing the CAMShift and Kalman filter algorithms.

You will find the code for this application in `chapter8/surveillance_demo/` of the code repository.

A brief digression – functional versus object-oriented programming

Although most programmers are either familiar (or work on a constant basis) with **Object-oriented Programming (OOP)**, I have found that, the more the years pass, the more I prefer **Functional Programming (FP)** solutions.

For those not familiar with the terminology, FP is a programming paradigm adopted by many languages that treats programs as the evaluation of mathematical functions, allows functions to return functions, and permits functions as arguments in a function. The strength of FP does not only reside in what it can do, but also in what it can avoid, or aims at avoiding side-effects and changing states. If the topic of functional programming has sparked an interest, make sure to check out languages such as Haskell, Clojure, or ML.

What is a side-effect in programming terms? You can define a side effect as any function that changes any value that does not depend on the function's input. Python, along with many other languages, is susceptible to causing side-effects because—much like, for example, JavaScript—it allows access to global variables (and sometimes this access to global variables can be accidental!).

Another major issue encountered with languages that are not purely functional is the fact that a function's result will change over time, depending on the state of the variables involved. If a function takes an object as an argument—for example—and the computation relies on the internal state of that object, the function will return different results according to the changes in the object's state. This is something that very typically happens in languages, such as C and C++, in functions where one or more of the arguments are references to objects.

Why this digression? Because so far I have illustrated concepts using mostly functions; I did not shy away from accessing global variables where this was the simplest and most robust approach. However, the next program we will examine will contain OOP. So why do I choose to adopt OOP while advocating FP? Because OpenCV has quite an opinionated approach, which makes it hard to implement a program with a purely functional or object-oriented approach.

For example, any drawing function, such as `cv2.rectangle` and `cv2.circle`, modifies the argument passed into it. This approach contravenes one of the cardinal rules of functional programming, which is to avoid side-effects and changing states.

Out of curiosity, you could—in Python—redeclare the API of these drawing functions in a way that is more FP-friendly. For example, you could rewrite `cv2.rectangle` like this:

```
def drawRect(frame, topLeft, bottomRight, color, thickness, fill =
    cv2.LINE_AA):
    newframe = frame.copy()
    cv2.rectangle(newframe, topLeft, bottomRight, color,
        thickness, fill)
    return newframe
```

This approach—while computationally more expensive due to the `copy()` operation—allows the explicit reassignment of a frame, like so:

```
frame = camera.read()
frame = drawRect(frame, (0,0), (10,10), (0, 255,0), 1)
```

To conclude this digression, I will reiterate a belief very often mentioned in all programming forums and resources: there is no such thing as the best language or paradigm, only the best tool for the job in hand.

So let's get back to our program and explore the implementation of a surveillance application, tracking moving objects in a video.

The Pedestrian class

The main rationale behind the creation of a Pedestrian class is the nature of the Kalman filter. The Kalman filter can predict the position of an object based on historical observations and correct the prediction based on the actual data, but it can only do that for one object.

As a consequence, we need one Kalman filter per object tracked.

So the Pedestrian class will act as a holder for a Kalman filter, a color histogram (calculated on the first detection of the object and used as a reference for the subsequent frames), and information about the region of interest, which will be used by the CAMShift algorithm (the track_window parameter).

Furthermore, we store the ID of each pedestrian for some fancy real-time info.

Let's take a look at the Pedestrian class:

```
class Pedestrian():
  """Pedestrian class

  each pedestrian is composed of a ROI, an ID and a Kalman filter
  so we create a Pedestrian class to hold the object state
  """
  def __init__(self, id, frame, track_window):
    """init the pedestrian object with track window coordinates"""
    # set up the roi
    self.id = int(id)
    x,y,w,h = track_window
    self.track_window = track_window
    self.roi = cv2.cvtColor(frame[y:y+h, x:x+w],
        cv2.COLOR_BGR2HSV)
    roi_hist = cv2.calcHist([self.roi], [0], None, [16], [0, 180])
    self.roi_hist = cv2.normalize(roi_hist, roi_hist, 0, 255,
        cv2.NORM_MINMAX)

    # set up the kalman
    self.kalman = cv2.KalmanFilter(4,2)
```

```python
        self.kalman.measurementMatrix =
            np.array([[1,0,0,0],[0,1,0,0]],np.float32)
        self.kalman.transitionMatrix =
            np.array([[1,0,1,0],[0,1,0,1],[0,0,1,0],[0,0,0,1]],
                np.float32)
        self.kalman.processNoiseCov =
            np.array([[1,0,0,0],[0,1,0,0],[0,0,1,0],[0,0,0,1]],
                np.float32) * 0.03
        self.measurement = np.array((2,1), np.float32)
        self.prediction = np.zeros((2,1), np.float32)
        self.term_crit = ( cv2.TERM_CRITERIA_EPS |
            cv2.TERM_CRITERIA_COUNT, 10, 1 )
        self.center = None
        self.update(frame)

    def __del__(self):
        print "Pedestrian %d destroyed" % self.id

    def update(self, frame):
        # print "updating %d " % self.id
        hsv = cv2.cvtColor(frame, cv2.COLOR_BGR2HSV)
        back_project = cv2.calcBackProject([hsv],[0],
            self.roi_hist,[0,180],1)

        if args.get("algorithm") == "c":
            ret, self.track_window = cv2.CamShift(back_project,
                self.track_window, self.term_crit)
            pts = cv2.boxPoints(ret)
            pts = np.int0(pts)
            self.center = center(pts)
            cv2.polylines(frame,[pts],True, 255,1)

        if not args.get("algorithm") or args.get("algorithm") == "m":
            ret, self.track_window = cv2.meanShift(back_project,
                self.track_window, self.term_crit)
            x,y,w,h = self.track_window
            self.center = center([[x,y],[x+w, y],[x,y+h],[x+w, y+h]])
            cv2.rectangle(frame, (x,y), (x+w, y+h), (255, 255, 0), 1)

        self.kalman.correct(self.center)
        prediction = self.kalman.predict()
        cv2.circle(frame, (int(prediction[0]), int(prediction[1])), 4,
            (0, 255, 0), -1)
        # fake shadow
```

```
cv2.putText(frame, "ID: %d -> %s" % (self.id, self.center),
    (11, (self.id + 1) * 25 + 1),
    font, 0.6,
    (0, 0, 0),
    1,
    cv2.LINE_AA)
# actual info
cv2.putText(frame, "ID: %d -> %s" % (self.id, self.center),
    (10, (self.id + 1) * 25),
    font, 0.6,
    (0, 255, 0),
    1,
    cv2.LINE_AA)
```

At the core of the program lies the background subtractor object, which lets us identify regions of interest corresponding to moving objects.

When the program starts, we take each of these regions and instantiate a `Pedestrian` class, passing the ID (a simple counter), and the frame and track window coordinates (so we can extract the **Region of Interest (ROI)**, and, from this, the HSV histogram of the ROI).

The constructor function (`__init__` in Python) is more or less an aggregation of all the previous concepts: given an ROI, we calculate its histogram, set up a Kalman filter, and associate it to a property (`self.kalman`) of the object.

In the `update` method, we pass the current frame and convert it to HSV so that we can calculate the back projection of the pedestrian's HSV histogram.

We then use either CAMShift or Meanshift (depending on the argument passed; Meanshift is the default if no arguments are passed) to track the movement of the pedestrian, and correct the Kalman filter for that pedestrian with the actual position.

We also draw both CAMShift/Meanshift (with a surrounding rectangle) and Kalman (with a dot), so you can observe Kalman and CAMShift/Meanshift go nearly hand in hand, except for sudden movements that cause Kalman to have to readjust.

Lastly, we print some pedestrian information on the top-left corner of the image.

The main program

Now that we have a `Pedestrian` class holding all specific information for each object, let's take a look at the main function in the program.

First, we load a video (it could be a webcam), and then we initialize a background subtractor, setting 20 frames as the frames affecting the background model:

```
history = 20
bs = cv2.createBackgroundSubtractorKNN(detectShadows = True)
bs.setHistory(history)
```

We also create the main display window, and then set up a pedestrians dictionary and a `firstFrame` flag, which we're going to use to allow a few frames for the background subtractor to build history, so it can better identify moving objects. To help with this, we also set up a frame counter:

```
cv2.namedWindow("surveillance")
  pedestrians = {}
  firstFrame = True
  frames = 0
```

Now we start the loop. We read camera frames (or video frames) one by one:

```
while True:
    print " ------------------- FRAME %d -------------------" %
        frames
    grabbed, frane = camera.read()
    if (grabbed is False):
      print "failed to grab frame."
      break

    ret, frame = camera.read()
```

We let `BackgroundSubtractorKNN` build the history for the background model, so we don't actually process the first 20 frames; we only pass them into the subtractor:

```
fgmask = bs.apply(frame)
# this is just to let the background subtractor build a bit of
    history
if frames < history:
  frames += 1
  continue
```

Then we process the frame with the approach explained earlier in the chapter, by applying a process of dilation and erosion on the foreground mask so as to obtain easily identifiable blobs and their bounding boxes. These are obviously moving objects in the frame:

```
th = cv2.threshold(fgmask.copy(), 127, 255,
    cv2.THRESH_BINARY)[1]
th = cv2.erode(th,
    cv2.getStructuringElement(cv2.MORPH_ELLIPSE, (3,3)),
        iterations = 2)
dilated = cv2.dilate(th,
    cv2.getStructuringElement(cv2.MORPH_ELLIPSE, (8,3)),
        iterations = 2)
image, contours, hier = cv2.findContours(dilated,
    cv2.RETR_EXTERNAL, cv2.CHAIN_APPROX_SIMPLE)
```

Once the contours are identified, we instantiate one pedestrian per contour for the first frame only (note that I set a minimum area for the contour to further denoise our detection):

```
counter = 0
for c in contours:
  if cv2.contourArea(c) > 500:
    (x,y,w,h) = cv2.boundingRect(c)
    cv2.rectangle(frame, (x,y), (x+w, y+h), (0, 255, 0), 1)
    # only create pedestrians in the first frame, then just
        follow the ones you have
    if firstFrame is True:
      pedestrians[counter] = Pedestrian(counter, frame,
        (x,y,w,h))
    counter += 1
```

Then, for each pedestrian detected, we perform an `update` method passing the current frame, which is needed in its original color space, because the pedestrian objects are responsible for drawing their own information (text and Meanshift/CAMShift rectangles, and Kalman filter tracking):

```
for i, p in pedestrians.iteritems():
    p.update(frame)
```

We set the `firstFrame` flag to `False`, so we don't instantiate any more pedestrians; we just keep track of the ones we have:

```
firstFrame = False
frames += 1
```

Finally, we show the result in the display window. The program can be exited by pressing the *Esc* key:

```
cv2.imshow("surveillance", frame)
if cv2.waitKey(110) & 0xff == 27:
    break

if __name__ == "__main__":
  main()
```

There you have it: CAMShift/Meanshift working in tandem with the Kalman filter to track moving objects. All being well, you should obtain a result similar to this:

In this screenshot, the blue rectangle is the CAMShift detection and the green rectangle is the Kalman filter prediction with its center at the blue circle.

Where do we go from here?

This program constitutes a basis for your application domain's needs. There are many improvements that can be made building on the program above to suit an application's additional requirements. Consider the following examples:

- You could destroy a pedestrian object if Kalman predicts its position to be outside the frame
- You could check whether each detected moving object is corresponding to existing pedestrian instances, and if not, create an instance for it
- You could train an SVM and operate classification on each moving object to establish whether or not the moving object is of the nature you intend to track (for instance, a dog might enter the scene but your application requires to only track humans)

Whatever your needs, hopefully this chapter will have provided you with the necessary knowledge to build applications that satisfy your requirements.

Summary

This chapter explored the vast and complex topic of video analysis and tracking objects.

We learned about video background subtraction with a basic motion detection technique that calculates frame differences, and then moved to more complex and efficient tools such as `BackgroundSubtractor`.

We then explored two very important video analysis algorithms: Meanshift and CAMShift. In the course of this, we talked in detail about color histograms and back projections. We also familiarized ourselves with the Kalman filter, and its usefulness in a computer vision context. Finally, we put all our knowledge together in a sample surveillance application, which tracks moving objects in a video.

Now that our foundation in OpenCV and machine learning is solidifying, we are ready to tackle artificial neural networks and dive deeper into artificial intelligence with OpenCV and Python in the next chapter.

9
Neural Networks with OpenCV – an Introduction

Machine learning is a branch of artificial intelligence, one that deals specifically with algorithms that enable a machine to recognize patterns and trends in data and successfully make predictions and classifications.

Many of the algorithms and techniques used by OpenCV to accomplish some of the more advanced tasks in computer vision are directly related to artificial intelligence and machine learning.

This chapter will introduce you to the Machine Learning concepts in OpenCV such as artificial neural networks. This is a gentle introduction that barely scratches the surface of a vast world, that of Machine Learning, which is continuously evolving.

Artificial neural networks

Let's start by defining **Artificial Neural Networks (ANN)** with a number of logical steps, rather than a classic monolithic sentence using obscure jargon with an even more obscure meaning.

First of all, an ANN is a **statistical model**. What is a statistical model? A statistical model is a pair of elements, namely the space S (a set of observations) and the probability P, where P is a distribution that approximates S (in other words, a function that would generate a set of observations that is very similar to S).

I like to think of P in two ways: as a simplification of a complex scenario, and as the function that generated S in the first place, or at the very least a set of observations very similar to S.

So ANNs are models that take a complex reality, simplify it, and deduce a function to (approximately) represent statistical observations one would expect from that reality, in mathematical form.

The next step in our journey towards comprehending ANNs is to understand how an ANN improves on the concept of a simple statistical model.

What if the function that generated the dataset is likely to take a large amount of (unknown) inputs?

The approach that ANNs take is to delegate work to a number of **neurons, nodes,** or **units**, each of which is capable of "approximating" the function that created the inputs. Approximation is mathematically the definition of a simpler function that approximates a more complex function, which enables us to define errors (relative to the application domain). Furthermore, for accuracy's sake, a network is generally recognized to be neural if the neurons or units are capable of approximating a nonlinear function.

Let's take a closer look at neurons.

Neurons and perceptrons

The **perceptron** is a concept that dates back to the 1950s, and (to put it simply) a perceptron is a function that takes a number of inputs and produces a single value.

Each of the inputs has an associated weight that signifies the importance of the input in the function. The sigmoid function produces a single value:

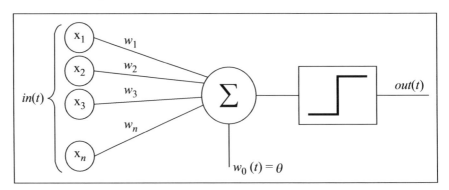

A sigmoid function is a term that indicates that the function produces either a 0 or 1 value. The discriminant is a threshold value; if the weighted sum of the inputs is greater than a certain threshold, the perceptron produces a binary classification of 1, otherwise 0.

How are these weights determined, and what do they represent?

Neurons are interconnected to each other, and each neuron's set of weights (these are just numerical parameters) defines the strength of the connection to other neurons. These weights are "adaptive", meaning they change in time according to a learning algorithm.

The structure of an ANN

Here's a visual representation of a neural network:

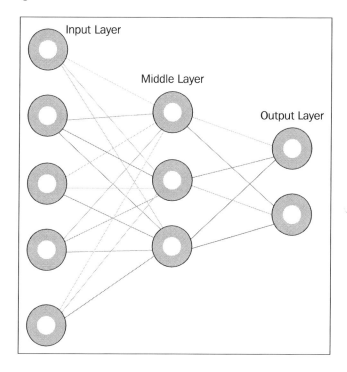

As you can see from the figure, there are three distinct layers in a neural network: **Input layer**, **Hidden layer** (or middle), and **Output layer**.

There can be more than one hidden layer; however, one hidden layer would be enough to resolve the majority of real-life problems.

Network layers by example

How do we determine the network's topology, and how many neurons to create for each layer? Let's make this determination layer by layer.

The input layer

The input layer defines the number of inputs into the network. For example, let's say you want to create an ANN, which will help you determine what animal you're looking at given a description of its attributes. Let's fix these attributes to weight, length, and teeth. That's a set of three attributes; our network will need to contain three input nodes.

The output layer

The output layer is equal to the number of classes we identified. Continuing with the preceding example of an animal classification network, we will arbitrarily set the output layer to 4, because we know we're going to deal with the following animals: dog, condor, dolphin, and dragon. If we feed in data for an animal that is not in one of these categories, the network will return the class most likely to resemble this unclassified animal.

The hidden layer

The hidden layer contains perceptrons. As mentioned, the vast majority of problems only require one hidden layer; mathematically speaking, there is no verified reason to have more than two hidden layers. We will, therefore, stick to one hidden layer and work with that.

There are a number of rules of thumb to determine the number of neurons contained in the hidden layer, but there is no hard-and-fast rule. The empirical way is your friend in this particular circumstance: test your network with different settings, and choose the one that fits best.

These are some of the most common rules used when building an ANN:

- The number of hidden neurons should be between the size of the input layer and the size of the output layer. If the difference between the input layer size and the output layer is large, it is my experience that a hidden layer size much closer to the output layer is preferable.

- For relatively small input layers, the number of hidden neurons is two-thirds the size of the input layer, plus the size of the output layer, or less than twice the size of the input layer.

One very important factor to keep in mind is **overfitting**. Overfitting occurs when there's such an inordinate amount of information contained in the hidden layer (for example, a disproportionate amount of neurons in the layer) compared to the information provided by the training data that classification is not very meaningful.

The larger the hidden layer, the more training information is required for the network to be trained properly. And, needless to say, this is going to lengthen the time required by the network to properly train.

So, following the second rules of thumb illustrated earlier, our network will have a hidden layer of size 8, just because after a few runs of the network, I found it to yield the best results. As a side note, the empirical approach is very much encouraged in the world of ANNs. The best network topology is related to the type of data fed to the network, so don't refrain from testing ANNs in a trial-and-error fashion.

In summary, our network has the following sizes:

- **Input**: 3
- **Hidden**: 8
- **Output**: 4

The learning algorithms

There are a number of learning algorithms used by ANNs, but we can identify three major ones:

- **Supervised learning**: With this algorithm, we want to obtain a function from the ANN, which describes the data we labeled. We know, a priori, the nature of this data, and we delegate to the ANN the process of finding a function that describes the data.

- **Unsupervised learning**: This algorithm differs from supervised learning; in this, the data is unlabeled. This implies that we don't have to select and label data, but it also means the ANN has a lot more work to do. The classification of the data is usually obtained through techniques such as (but not only) clustering, which we explored in *Chapter 7, Detecting and Recognizing Objects.*

- **Reinforcement learning**: Reinforcement learning is a little more complex. A system receives an input; a decision-making mechanism determines an action, which is performed and scored (success/failure and grades in between); and finally the input and the action are paired with their score, so the system learns to repeat or change the action to be performed for a certain input or state.

Now that we have a general idea of what ANNs are, let's see how OpenCV implements them, and how to put them to good use. Finally, we'll work our way up to a full blown application, in which we will attempt to recognize handwritten digits.

ANNs in OpenCV

Unsurprisingly, ANNs reside in the `ml` module of OpenCV.

Let's examine a dummy example, as a gentle introduction to ANNs:

```
import cv2
import numpy as np

ann = cv2.ml.ANN_MLP_create()
ann.setLayerSizes(np.array([9, 5, 9], dtype=np.uint8))
ann.setTrainMethod(cv2.ml.ANN_MLP_BACKPROP)

ann.train(np.array([[1.2, 1.3, 1.9, 2.2, 2.3, 2.9, 3.0, 3.2,
    3.3]], dtype=np.float32),
    cv2.ml.ROW_SAMPLE,
    np.array([[0, 0, 0, 0, 0, 1, 0, 0, 0]], dtype=np.float32))

print ann.predict(np.array([[1.4, 1.5, 1.2, 2., 2.5, 2.8, 3., 3.1,
    3.8]], dtype=np.float32))
```

First, we create an ANN:

```
ann = cv2.ml.ANN_MLP_create()
```

You may wonder about the `MLP` acronym in the function name; it stands for **multilayer perceptron**. By now, you should know what a perceptron is.

After creating the network, we need to set its topology:

```
ann.setLayerSizes(np.array([9, 5, 9], dtype=np.uint8))
ann.setTrainMethod(cv2.ml.ANN_MLP_BACKPROP)
```

The layer sizes are defined by the NumPy array that is passed into the `setLayerSizes` method. The first element sets the size of the input layer, the last element sets the size of the output layer, and all intermediary elements define the size of the hidden layers.

We then set the train method to be backpropagation. There are two choices here: BACKPROP and RPROP.

Both BACKPROP and RPROP are backpropagation algorithms — in simple terms, algorithms that have an effect on weights based on errors in classification.

These two algorithms work in the context of supervised learning, which is what we are using in the example. How can we tell this particular detail? Look at the next statement:

```
ann.train(np.array([[1.2, 1.3, 1.9, 2.2, 2.3, 2.9, 3.0, 3.2,
    3.3]], dtype=np.float32),
    cv2.ml.ROW_SAMPLE,
    np.array([[0, 0, 0, 0, 0, 1, 0, 0, 0]], dtype=np.float32))
```

You should notice a number of details. The method looks extremely similar to the train() method of support vector machine. The method contains three parameters: samples, layout, and responses. Only samples is the required parameter; the other two are optional.

This reveals the following information:

- First, ANN, like SVM, is an OpenCV StatModel (**statistical model**); train and predict are the methods inherited from the base StatModel class.

- Second, a statistical model trained with only samples is adopting an unsupervised learning algorithm. If we provide layout and responses, we're in a supervised learning context.

As we're using ANNs, we can specify the type of back propagation algorithm we're going to use (BACKPROP or RPROP), because — as we said — we're in a supervised learning environment.

So what is back propagation? Back propagation is a two-phase algorithm that calculates the error of predictions and updates in both directions of the network (the input and output layers); it then updates the neuron weights accordingly.

Let's train the ANN; as we specified an input layer of size 9, we need to provide 9 inputs, and 9 outputs to reflect the size of the output layer:

```
ann.train(np.array([[1.2, 1.3, 1.9, 2.2, 2.3, 2.9, 3.0, 3.2,
    3.3]], dtype=np.float32),
    cv2.ml.ROW_SAMPLE,
    np.array([[0, 0, 0, 0, 0, 1, 0, 0, 0]], dtype=np.float32))
```

The structure of the response is simply an array of zeros, with a 1 value in the position indicating the class we want to associate the input with. In our preceding example, we indicated that the specified input array corresponds to class 5 (classes are zero-indexed) of classes 0 to 8.

Lastly, we perform classification:

```
print ann.predict(np.array([[1.4, 1.5, 1.2, 2., 2.5, 2.8, 3., 3.1,
   3.8]], dtype=np.float32))
```

This will yield the following result:

```
(5.0, array([[-0.06419383, -0.13360272, -0.1681568 , -0.18708915,
   0.0970564 ,
   0.89237726, 0.05093023, 0.17537238, 0.13388439]],
     dtype=float32))
```

This means that the provided input was classified as belonging to class 5. This is only a dummy example and the classification is pretty meaningless; however, the network behaved correctly. In this code, we only provided one training record for class 5, so the network classified a new input as belonging to class 5.

As you may have guessed, the output of a prediction is a tuple, with the first value being the class and the second being an array containing the probabilities for each class. The predicted class will have the highest value. Let's move on to a slightly more useful example: animal classification.

ANN-imal classification

Picking up from where we left off, let's illustrate a very simple example of an ANN that attempts to classify animals based on their statistics (weight, length, and teeth). My intent is to describe a mock real-life scenario to improve our understanding of ANNs before we start applying it to computer vision and, specifically, OpenCV:

```
import cv2
import numpy as np
from random import randint

animals_net = cv2.ml.ANN_MLP_create()
animals_net.setTrainMethod(cv2.ml.ANN_MLP_RPROP |
   cv2.ml.ANN_MLP_UPDATE_WEIGHTS)
animals_net.setActivationFunction(cv2.ml.ANN_MLP_SIGMOID_SYM)
animals_net.setLayerSizes(np.array([3, 8, 4]))
animals_net.setTermCriteria(( cv2.TERM_CRITERIA_EPS |
   cv2.TERM_CRITERIA_COUNT, 10, 1 ))

"""Input arrays
weight, length, teeth
"""

"""Output arrays
```

```
dog, eagle, dolphin and dragon
"""

def dog_sample():
  return [randint(5, 20), 1, randint(38, 42)]

def dog_class():
  return [1, 0, 0, 0]

def condor_sample():
  return [randint(3,13), 3, 0]

def condor_class():
  return [0, 1, 0, 0]

def dolphin_sample():
  return [randint(30, 190), randint(5, 15), randint(80, 100)]

def dolphin_class():
  return [0, 0, 1, 0]

def dragon_sample():
  return [randint(1200, 1800), randint(15, 40), randint(110, 180)]

def dragon_class():
  return [0, 0, 0, 1]

SAMPLES = 5000
for x in range(0, SAMPLES):
  print "Samples %d/%d" % (x, SAMPLES)
  animals_net.train(np.array([dog_sample()], dtype=np.float32),
    cv2.ml.ROW_SAMPLE, np.array([dog_class()], dtype=np.float32))
  animals_net.train(np.array([condor_sample()], dtype=np.float32),
    cv2.ml.ROW_SAMPLE, np.array([condor_class()],
      dtype=np.float32))
  animals_net.train(np.array([dolphin_sample()],
    dtype=np.float32), cv2.ml.ROW_SAMPLE,
      np.array([dolphin_class()], dtype=np.float32))
  animals_net.train(np.array([dragon_sample()], dtype=np.float32),
    cv2.ml.ROW_SAMPLE, np.array([dragon_class()],
      dtype=np.float32))

print animals_net.predict(np.array([dog_sample()],
  dtype=np.float32))
```

```
print animals_net.predict(np.array([condor_sample()],
  dtype=np.float32))
print animals_net.predict(np.array([dragon_sample()],
  dtype=np.float32))
```

There are a good few differences between this example and the dummy example, so let's examine them in order.

First, the usual imports. Then, we import `randint`, just because we want to generate some relatively random data:

```
import cv2
import numpy as np
from random import randint
```

Then, we create the ANN. This time, we specify the `train` method to be resilient back propagation (an improved version of back propagation) and the activation function to be a sigmoid function:

```
animals_net = cv2.ml.ANN_MLP_create()
animals_net.setTrainMethod(cv2.ml.ANN_MLP_RPROP |
  cv2.ml.ANN_MLP_UPDATE_WEIGHTS)
animals_net.setActivationFunction(cv2.ml.ANN_MLP_SIGMOID_SYM)
animals_net.setLayerSizes(np.array([3, 8, 4]))
```

Also, we specify the termination criteria similarly to the way we did in the CAMShift algorithm in the previous chapter:

```
animals_net.setTermCriteria(( cv2.TERM_CRITERIA_EPS |
  cv2.TERM_CRITERIA_COUNT, 10, 1 ))
```

Now we need some data. We're not really so much interested in representing animals accurately, as requiring a bunch of records to be used as training data. So we basically define four sample creation functions and four classification functions that will help us train the network:

```
"""Input arrays
weight, length, teeth
"""

"""Output arrays
dog, eagle, dolphin and dragon
"""

def dog_sample():
```

```
    return [randint(5, 20), 1, randint(38, 42)]

def dog_class():
    return [1, 0, 0, 0]

def condor_sample():
    return [randint(3,13), 3, 0]

def condor_class():
    return [0, 1, 0, 0]

def dolphin_sample():
    return [randint(30, 190), randint(5, 15), randint(80, 100)]

def dolphin_class():
    return [0, 0, 1, 0]

def dragon_sample():
    return [randint(1200, 1800), randint(15, 40), randint(110, 180)]

def dragon_class():
    return [0, 0, 0, 1]
```

Let's proceed with the creation of our fake animal data; we'll create 5,000 samples per class:

```
SAMPLES = 5000
for x in range(0, SAMPLES):
    print "Samples %d/%d" % (x, SAMPLES)
    animals_net.train(np.array([dog_sample()], dtype=np.float32),
        cv2.ml.ROW_SAMPLE, np.array([dog_class()], dtype=np.float32))
animals_net.train(np.array([condor_sample()], dtype=np.float32),
    cv2.ml.ROW_SAMPLE, np.array([condor_class()], dtype=np.float32))
    animals_net.train(np.array([dolphin_sample()],
        dtype=np.float32), cv2.ml.ROW_SAMPLE,
        np.array([dolphin_class()], dtype=np.float32))
        animals_net.train(np.array([dragon_sample()],
            dtype=np.float32),        cv2.ml.ROW_SAMPLE,
            np.array([dragon_class()], dtype=np.float32))
```

In the end, we print the results that yield the following code:

```
(1.0, array([[ 1.49817729,  1.60551953, -1.56444871,
  -0.04313202]], dtype=float32))
(1.0, array([[ 1.49817729,  1.60551953, -1.56444871,
  -0.04313202]], dtype=float32))
(3.0, array([[-1.54576635, -1.68725526,  1.6469276 ,
  2.23223686]], dtype=float32))
```

From these results, we deduce the following:

- The network got two out of three samples correct, which is not perfect but serves as a good example to illustrate the importance of all the elements involved in building and training an ANN. The size of the input layer is very important to create diversification between the different classes. In our case, we only had three statistics and there is a relative overlapping in features.

- The size of the hidden layer needs to be tested. You will find that increasing neurons may improve accuracy to a point, and then it will overfit, unless you start compensating with enormous amounts of data: the number of training records. Definitely, avoid having too few records or feeding a lot of identical records as the ANN won't learn much from them.

Training epochs

Another important concept in training ANNs is the idea of epochs. A training epoch is an iteration through the training data, after which the data is tested for classification. Most ANNs train over several epochs; you'll find that some of the most common examples of ANNs, classifying handwritten digits, will have the training data iterated several hundred times.

I personally suggest you spend a lot of time playing with ANNs and the number of epochs, until you reach convergence, which means that further iterations will no longer improve (at least not noticeably) the accuracy of the results.

The preceding example can be modified as follows to leverage epochs:

```
def record(sample, classification):
    return (np.array([sample], dtype=np.float32),
        np.array([classification], dtype=np.float32))

records = []
RECORDS = 5000
for x in range(0, RECORDS):
    records.append(record(dog_sample(), dog_class()))
```

```
records.append(record(condor_sample(), condor_class()))
records.append(record(dolphin_sample(), dolphin_class()))
records.append(record(dragon_sample(), dragon_class()))

EPOCHS = 5
for e in range(0, EPOCHS):
  print "Epoch %d:" % e
  for t, c in records:
    animals_net.train(t, cv2.ml.ROW_SAMPLE, c)
```

Then, do some tests, starting with the dog class:

```
dog_results = 0
for x in range(0, 100):
  clas = int(animals_net.predict(np.array([dog_sample()],
    dtype=np.float32))[0])
  print "class: %d" % clas
  if (clas) == 0:
    dog_results += 1
```

Repeat over all classes and output the results:

```
print "Dog accuracy: %f" % (dog_results)
print "condor accuracy: %f" % (condor_results)
print "dolphin accuracy: %f" % (dolphin_results)
print "dragon accuracy: %f" % (dragon_results)
```

Finally, we obtain the following results:

```
Dog accuracy: 100.000000%
condor accuracy: 0.000000%
dolphin accuracy: 0.000000%
dragon accuracy: 92.000000%
```

Consider the fact that we're only playing with toy/fake data and the size of training data/training iterations; this teaches us quite a lot. We can diagnose the ANN as overfitting towards certain classes, so it's important to improve the quality of the data you feed into the training process.

All that said, time for a real-life example: handwritten digit recognition.

Handwritten digit recognition with ANNs

The world of Machine Learning is vast and mostly unexplored, and ANNs are but one of the many concepts related to Machine Learning, which is one of the many subdisciplines of Artificial Intelligence. For the purpose of this chapter, we will only be exploring the concept of ANNs in the context of OpenCV. It is by no means an exhaustive treatise on the subject of Artificial Intelligence.

Ultimately, we're interested in seeing ANNs work in the real world. So let's go ahead and make it happen.

MNIST – the handwritten digit database

One of the most popular resources on the Web for the training of classifiers dealing with OCR and handwritten character recognition is the MNIST database, publicly available at http://yann.lecun.com/exdb/mnist/.

This particular database is a freely available resource to kick-start the creation of a program that utilizes ANNs to recognize handwritten digits.

Customized training data

It is always possible to build your own training data. It will take a little bit of patience but it's fairly easy; collect a vast number of handwritten digits and create images containing a single digit, making sure all the images are the same size and in grayscale.

After this, you will have to create a mechanism that keeps a training sample in sync with the expected classification.

The initial parameters

Let's take a look at the individual layers in the network:

- Input layer
- Hidden layer
- Output layer

The input layer

Since we're going to utilize the MNIST database, the input layer will have a size of 784 input nodes: that's because MNIST samples are 28x28 pixel images, which means 784 pixels.

The hidden layer

As we have seen, there's no hard-and-fast rule for the size of the hidden layer, I've found—through several attempts—that 50 to 60 nodes yields the best result while not necessitating an inordinate amount of training data.

You can increase the size of the hidden layer with the amount of data, but beyond a certain point, there will be no advantage to that; you will also have to be prepared for your network to take hours to train (the more hidden neurons, the longer it takes to train the network).

The output layer

The output layer will have a size of 10. This should not be a surprise as we want to classify 10 digits (0-9).

Training epochs

We will initially use the entire set of the `train` data from MNIST, which consists of over 60,000 handwritten images, half of which were written by US government employees, and the other half by high-school students. That's a lot of data, so we won't need more than one epoch to achieve an acceptably high accuracy on detection.

From there on, it is up to you to train the network iteratively on the same `train` data, and my suggestion is that you use an accuracy test, and find the epoch at which the accuracy "peaks". By doing so, you will have a precise measurement of the highest possible accuracy achieved by your network given its current configuration.

Other parameters

We will use a sigmoid activation function, **Resilient Back Propagation (RPROP)**, and extend the termination criteria for each calculation to 20 iterations instead of 10, like we did for every other operation in this book that involved `cv2.TermCriteria`.

Important notes on train data and ANNs libraries

Exploring the Internet for sources, I found an amazing article by Michael Nielsen at `http://neuralnetworksanddeeplearning.com/chap1.html`, which illustrates how to write an ANN library from scratch, and the code for this library is freely available on GitHub at `https://github.com/mnielsen/neural-networks-and-deep-learning`; this is the source code for a book, *Neural Networks and Deep Learning*, by Michael Nielsen.

In the `data` folder, you will find a `pickle` file, signifying data that has been saved to disk through the popular Python library, `cPickle`, which makes loading and saving the Python data a trivial task.

This pickle file is a `cPickle` library-serialized version of the MNIST data and, as it is so useful and ready to work with, I strongly suggest you use that. Nothing stops you from loading the MNIST dataset but the process of deserializing the training data is quite tedious and — strictly speaking — outside the remit of this book.

Second, I would like to point out that OpenCV is not the only Python library that allows you to use ANNs, not by any stretch of the imagination. The Web is full of alternatives that I strongly encourage you to try out, most notably **PyBrain**, a library called **Lasagna** (which — as an Italian — I find exceptionally attractive) and many custom-written implementations, such as the aforementioned Michael Nielsen's implementation.

Enough introductory details, though. Let's get going.

Mini-libraries

Setting up an ANN in OpenCV is not difficult, but you will almost definitely find yourself training your network countless times, in search of that elusive percentage point that boosts the accuracy of your results.

To automate this as much as possible, we will build a mini-library that wraps the OpenCV's native implementation of ANNs and lets us rerun and retrain the network easily.

Here's an example of a wrapper library:

```
import cv2
import cPickle
import numpy as np
import gzip

def load_data():
  mnist = gzip.open('./data/mnist.pkl.gz', 'rb')
  training_data, classification_data, test_data =
    cPickle.load(mnist)
  mnist.close()
  return (training_data, classification_data, test_data)

def wrap_data():
  tr_d, va_d, te_d = load_data()
  training_inputs = [np.reshape(x, (784, 1)) for x in tr_d[0]]
```

```
    training_results = [vectorized_result(y) for y in tr_d[1]]
    training_data = zip(training_inputs, training_results)
    validation_inputs = [np.reshape(x, (784, 1)) for x in va_d[0]]
    validation_data = zip(validation_inputs, va_d[1])
    test_inputs = [np.reshape(x, (784, 1)) for x in te_d[0]]
    test_data = zip(test_inputs, te_d[1])
    return (training_data, validation_data, test_data)

def vectorized_result(j):
  e = np.zeros((10, 1))
  e[j] = 1.0
  return e

def create_ANN(hidden = 20):
  ann = cv2.ml.ANN_MLP_create()
  ann.setLayerSizes(np.array([784, hidden, 10]))
  ann.setTrainMethod(cv2.ml.ANN_MLP_RPROP)
  ann.setActivationFunction(cv2.ml.ANN_MLP_SIGMOID_SYM)
  ann.setTermCriteria(( cv2.TERM_CRITERIA_EPS |
    cv2.TERM_CRITERIA_COUNT, 20, 1 ))
  return ann

def train(ann, samples = 10000, epochs = 1):
  tr, val, test = wrap_data()


  for x in xrange(epochs):
    counter = 0
    for img in tr:

      if (counter > samples):
        break
      if (counter % 1000 == 0):
        print "Epoch %d: Trained %d/%d" % (x, counter, samples)
      counter += 1
      data, digit = img
      ann.train(np.array([data.ravel()], dtype=np.float32),
        cv2.ml.ROW_SAMPLE, np.array([digit.ravel()],
          dtype=np.float32))
    print "Epoch %d complete" % x
  return ann, test

def test(ann, test_data):
  sample = np.array(test_data[0][0].ravel(),
    dtype=np.float32).reshape(28, 28)
```

```
    cv2.imshow("sample", sample)
    cv2.waitKey()
    print ann.predict(np.array([test_data[0][0].ravel()],
      dtype=np.float32))

def predict(ann, sample):
  resized = sample.copy()
  rows, cols = resized.shape
  if (rows != 28 or cols != 28) and rows * cols > 0:
    resized = cv2.resize(resized, (28, 28), interpolation =
      cv2.INTER_CUBIC)
  return ann.predict(np.array([resized.ravel()],
    dtype=np.float32))
```

Let's examine it in order. First, the `load_data`, `wrap_data`, and `vectorized_result` functions are included in Michael Nielsen's code for loading the `pickle` file.

It's a relatively straightforward loading of a `pickle` file. Most notably, though, the loaded data has been split into the `train` and `test` data. Both `train` and `test` data are arrays containing two-element tuples: the first one is the data itself; the second one is the expected classification. So we can use the `train` data to train the ANN and the `test` data to evaluate its accuracy.

The `vectorized_result` function is a very clever function that—given an expected classification—creates a 10-element array of zeros, setting a single 1 for the expected result. This 10-element array, you may have guessed, will be used as a classification for the output layer.

The first ANN-related function is `create_ANN`:

```
def create_ANN(hidden = 20):
  ann = cv2.ml.ANN_MLP_create()
  ann.setLayerSizes(np.array([784, hidden, 10]))
  ann.setTrainMethod(cv2.ml.ANN_MLP_RPROP)
  ann.setActivationFunction(cv2.ml.ANN_MLP_SIGMOID_SYM)
  ann.setTermCriteria(( cv2.TERM_CRITERIA_EPS |
    cv2.TERM_CRITERIA_COUNT, 20, 1 ))
  return ann
```

This function creates an ANN specifically geared towards handwritten digit recognition with MNIST, by specifying layer sizes as illustrated in the *Initial parameters* section.

We now need a training function:

```
def train(ann, samples = 10000, epochs = 1):
  tr, val, test = wrap_data()


  for x in xrange(epochs):
    counter = 0
    for img in tr:

      if (counter > samples):
        break
      if (counter % 1000 == 0):
        print "Epoch %d: Trained %d/%d" % (x, counter, samples)
      counter += 1
      data, digit = img
      ann.train(np.array([data.ravel()], dtype=np.float32),
        cv2.ml.ROW_SAMPLE, np.array([digit.ravel()],
          dtype=np.float32))
    print "Epoch %d complete" % x
  return ann, test
```

Again, this is quite simple: given a number of samples and training epochs, we load the data, and then iterate through the samples an x-number-of-epochs times.

The important section of this function is the deconstruction of the single training record into the `train` data and an expected classification, which is then passed into the ANN.

To do so, we utilize the `numpy` array function, `ravel()`, which takes an array of any shape and "flattens" it into a single-row array. So, for example, consider this array:

```
data = [[ 1, 2, 3], [4, 5, 6], [7, 8, 9]]
```

The preceding array once "raveled", becomes the following array:

```
    [1, 2, 3, 4, 5, 6, 7, 8, 9]
```

This is the format that OpenCV's ANN expects data to look like in its `train()` method.

Finally, we return both the `network` and `test` data. We could have just returned the data, but having the `test` data at hand for accuracy checking is quite useful.

The last function we need is a `predict()` function to wrap ANN's own `predict()` method:

```
def predict(ann, sample):
  resized = sample.copy()
  rows, cols = resized.shape
  if (rows != 28 or cols != 28) and rows * cols > 0:
    resized = cv2.resize(resized, (28, 28), interpolation =
      cv2.INTER_CUBIC)
  return ann.predict(np.array([resized.ravel()],
    dtype=np.float32))
```

This function takes an ANN and a sample image; it operates a minimum of "sanitization" by making sure the shape of the data is as expected and resizing it if it's not, and then raveling it for a successful prediction.

The file I created also contains a `test` function to verify that the network works and it displays the sample provided for classification.

The main file

This whole chapter has been an introductory journey leading us to this point. In fact, many of the techniques we're going to use are from previous chapters, so in a way the entire book has led us to this point. So let's put all our knowledge to good use.

Let's take an initial look at the file, and then decompose it for a better understanding:

```
import cv2
import numpy as np
import digits_ann as ANN

def inside(r1, r2):
  x1,y1,w1,h1 = r1
  x2,y2,w2,h2 = r2
  if (x1 > x2) and (y1 > y2) and (x1+w1 < x2+w2) and (y1+h1 < y2 +
    h2):
    return True
  else:
    return False

def wrap_digit(rect):
  x, y, w, h = rect
  padding = 5
  hcenter = x + w/2
  vcenter = y + h/2
```

```
  if (h > w):
    w = h
    x = hcenter - (w/2)
  else:
    h = w
    y = vcenter - (h/2)
  return (x-padding, y-padding, w+padding, h+padding)

ann, test_data = ANN.train(ANN.create_ANN(56), 20000)
font = cv2.FONT_HERSHEY_SIMPLEX

path = "./images/numbers.jpg"
img = cv2.imread(path, cv2.IMREAD_UNCHANGED)
bw = cv2.cvtColor(img, cv2.COLOR_BGR2GRAY)
bw = cv2.GaussianBlur(bw, (7,7), 0)
ret, thbw = cv2.threshold(bw, 127, 255, cv2.THRESH_BINARY_INV)
thbw = cv2.erode(thbw, np.ones((2,2), np.uint8), iterations = 2)
image, cntrs, hier = cv2.findContours(thbw.copy(), cv2.RETR_TREE,
  cv2.CHAIN_APPROX_SIMPLE)

rectangles = []

for c in cntrs:
  r = x,y,w,h = cv2.boundingRect(c)
  a = cv2.contourArea(c)
  b = (img.shape[0]-3) * (img.shape[1] - 3)

  is_inside = False
  for q in rectangles:
    if inside(r, q):
      is_inside = True
      break
  if not is_inside:
    if not a == b:
      rectangles.append(r)

for r in rectangles:
  x,y,w,h = wrap_digit(r)
  cv2.rectangle(img, (x,y), (x+w, y+h), (0, 255, 0), 2)
  roi = thbw[y:y+h, x:x+w]

  try:
    digit_class = int(ANN.predict(ann, roi.copy())[0])
  except:
```

```
      continue
    cv2.putText(img, "%d" % digit_class, (x, y-1), font, 1, (0, 255,
      0))

  cv2.imshow("thbw", thbw)
  cv2.imshow("contours", img)
  cv2.imwrite("sample.jpg", img)
  cv2.waitKey()
```

After the initial usual imports, we import the mini-library we created, which is stored in `digits_ann.py`.

I find it good practice to define functions at the top of the file, so let's examine those. The `inside()` function determines whether a rectangle is entirely contained in another rectangle:

```
def inside(r1, r2):
  x1,y1,w1,h1 = r1
  x2,y2,w2,h2 = r2
  if (x1 > x2) and (y1 > y2) and (x1+w1 < x2+w2) and (y1+h1 < y2 +
    h2):
    return True
  else:
    return False
```

The `wrap_digit()` function takes a rectangle that surrounds a digit, turns it into a square, and centers it on the digit itself, with 5-point padding to make sure the digit is entirely contained in it:

```
def wrap_digit(rect):
  x, y, w, h = rect
  padding = 5
  hcenter = x + w/2
  vcenter = y + h/2
  if (h > w):
    w = h
    x = hcenter - (w/2)
  else:
    h = w
    y = vcenter - (h/2)
  return (x-padding, y-padding, w+padding, h+padding)
```

The point of this function will become clearer later on; let's not dwell on it too much at the moment.

Now, let's create the network. We will use 58 hidden nodes, and train over 20,000 samples:

```
ann, test_data = ANN.train(ANN.create_ANN(58), 20000)
```

This is good enough for a preliminary test to keep the training time down to a minute or two (depending on the processing power of your machine). The ideal is to use the full set of training data (50,000), and iterate through it several times, until some convergence is reached (as we discussed earlier, the accuracy "peak"). You would do this by calling the following function:

```
ann, test_data = ANN.train(ANN.create_ANN(100), 50000, 30)
```

We can now prepare the data to test. To do that, we're going to load an image, and clean up a little:

```
path = "./images/numbers.jpg"
img = cv2.imread(path, cv2.IMREAD_UNCHANGED)
bw = cv2.cvtColor(img, cv2.COLOR_BGR2GRAY)
bw = cv2.GaussianBlur(bw, (7,7), 0)
```

Now that we have a grayscale smoothed image, we can apply a threshold and some morphology operations to make sure the numbers are properly standing out from the background and relatively cleaned up for irregularities, which might throw the prediction operation off:

```
ret, thbw = cv2.threshold(bw, 127, 255, cv2.THRESH_BINARY_INV)
thbw = cv2.erode(thbw, np.ones((2,2), np.uint8), iterations = 2)
```

 Note the threshold flag, which is for an inverse binary threshold: as the samples of the MNIST database are white on black (and not black on white), we turn the image into a black background with white numbers.

After the morphology operation, we need to identify and separate each number in the picture. To do this, we first identify the contours in the image:

```
image, cntrs, hier = cv2.findContours(thbw.copy(), cv2.RETR_TREE,
    cv2.CHAIN_APPROX_SIMPLE)
```

Then, we iterate through the contours, and discard all the rectangles that are entirely contained in other rectangles; we only append to the list of good rectangles the ones that are not contained in other rectangles and are also not as wide as the image itself. In some of the tests, `findContours` yielded the entire image as a contour itself, which meant no other rectangle passed the `inside` test:

```
rectangles = []

for c in cntrs:
    r = x,y,w,h = cv2.boundingRect(c)
    a = cv2.contourArea(c)
    b = (img.shape[0]-3) * (img.shape[1] - 3)

    is_inside = False
    for q in rectangles:
        if inside(r, q):
            is_inside = True
            break
    if not is_inside:
        if not a == b:
            rectangles.append(r)
```

Now that we have a list of good rectangles, we can iterate through them and define a region of interest for each of the rectangles we identified:

```
for r in rectangles:
    x,y,w,h = wrap_digit(r)
```

This is where the `wrap_digit()` function we defined at the beginning of the program comes into play: we need to pass a square region of interest to the predictor function; if we simply resized a rectangle into a square, we'd ruin our test data.

You may wonder why think of the number one. A rectangle surrounding the number one would be very narrow, especially if it has been drawn without too much of a lean to either side. If you simply resized it to a square, you would "fatten" the number one in such a way that nearly the entire square would turn black, rendering the prediction impossible. Instead, we want to create a square around the identified number, which is exactly what `wrap_digit()` does.

This approach is quick-and-dirty; it allows us to draw a square around a number and simultaneously pass that square as a region of interest for the prediction. A purer approach would be to take the original rectangle and "center" it into a square numpy array with rows and columns equal to the larger of the two dimensions of the original rectangle. The reason for this is you will notice that some of the square will include tiny bits of adjacent numbers, which can throw the prediction off. With a square created from a np.zeros() function, no impurities will be accidentally dragged in:

```
cv2.rectangle(img, (x,y), (x+w, y+h), (0, 255, 0), 2)
roi = thbw[y:y+h, x:x+w]

try:
    digit_class = int(ANN.predict(ann, roi.copy())[0])
except:
    continue
cv2.putText(img, "%d" % digit_class, (x, y-1), font, 1, (0, 255,
    0))
```

Once the prediction for the square region is complete, we draw it on the original image:

```
cv2.imshow("thbw", thbw)
cv2.imshow("contours", img)
cv2.imwrite("sample.jpg", img)
cv2.waitKey()
```

And that's it! The final result will look similar to this:

Possible improvements and potential applications

We have illustrated how to build an ANN, feed it training data, and use it for classification. There are a number of aspects we can improve, depending on the task at hand, and a number of potential applications of our new-found knowledge.

Improvements

There are a number of improvements that can be applied to this approach, some of which we have already discussed:

- For example, you could enlarge your dataset and iterate more times, until a performance peak is reached

- You could also experiment with the several activation functions (`cv2.ml.ANN_MLP_SIGMOID_SYM` is not the only one; there is also `cv2.ml.ANN_MLP_IDENTITY` and `cv2.ml.ANN_MLP_GAUSSIAN`)

- You could utilize different training flags (`cv2.ml.ANN_MLP_UPDATE_WEIGHTS`, `cv2.ml.ANN_MLP_NO_INPUT_SCALE`, `cv2.ml.ANN_MLP_NO_OUTPUT_SCALE`), and training methods (back propagation or resilient back propagation)

Aside from that, bear in mind one of the mantras of software development: there is no single best technology, there is only the best tool for the job at hand. So, careful analysis of the application requirements will lead you to the best choices of parameters. For example, not everyone draws digits the same way. In fact, you will even find that some countries draw numbers in a slightly different way.

The MNIST database was compiled in the US, in which the number seven is drawn like the character 7. But you will find that the number 7 in Europe is often drawn with a small horizontal line half way through the diagonal portion of the number, which was introduced to distinguish it from the number 1.

For a more detailed overview of regional handwriting variations, check the Wikipedia article on the subject, which is a good introduction, available at `https://en.wikipedia.org/wiki/Regional_handwriting_variation`.

This means the MNIST database has limited accuracy when applied to European handwriting; some numbers will be classified more accurately than others. So you may end up creating your own dataset. In almost all circumstances, it is preferable to utilize the `train` data that's relevant and belongs to the current application domain.

Finally, remember that once you're happy with the accuracy of your network, you can always save it and reload it later, so it can be utilized in third-party applications without having to train the ANN every time.

Potential applications

The preceding program is only the foundation of a handwriting recognition application. Straightaway, you can quickly extend the earlier approach to videos and detect handwritten digits in real-time, or you could train your ANN to recognize the entire alphabet for a full-blown OCR system.

Car registration plate detection seems like an obvious extension of the lessons learned to this point, and it should be an even easier domain to work with, as registration plates use consistent characters.

Also, for your own edification or business purposes, you may try to build a classifier with ANNs and plain SVMs (with feature detectors such as SIFT) and see how they benchmark.

Summary

In this chapter, we scratched the surface of the vast and fascinating world of ANNs, focusing on OpenCV's implementation of it. We learned about the structure of ANNs, and how to design a network topology based on application requirements.

Finally, we utilized various concepts that we explored in the previous chapters to build a handwritten digit recognition application.

To boldly go...

I hope you enjoyed the journey through the Python bindings for OpenCV 3. Although covering OpenCV 3 would take a series of books, we explored very fascinating and futuristic concepts, and I encourage you to get in touch and let me and the OpenCV community know what your next groundbreaking computer-vision-based project is!

Index

binary installers, using 3, 4
CMake , using 4-7
compilers, using 5-7
installation on 2, 3
window size 90

Y

Yale face database (Yalefaces)
URL 98

Thank you for buying
Learning OpenCV 3 Computer Vision with Python
Second Edition

About Packt Publishing

Packt, pronounced 'packed', published its first book, *Mastering phpMyAdmin for Effective MySQL Management*, in April 2004, and subsequently continued to specialize in publishing highly focused books on specific technologies and solutions.

Our books and publications share the experiences of your fellow IT professionals in adapting and customizing today's systems, applications, and frameworks. Our solution-based books give you the knowledge and power to customize the software and technologies you're using to get the job done. Packt books are more specific and less general than the IT books you have seen in the past. Our unique business model allows us to bring you more focused information, giving you more of what you need to know, and less of what you don't.

Packt is a modern yet unique publishing company that focuses on producing quality, cutting-edge books for communities of developers, administrators, and newbies alike. For more information, please visit our website at www.packtpub.com.

About Packt Open Source

In 2010, Packt launched two new brands, Packt Open Source and Packt Enterprise, in order to continue its focus on specialization. This book is part of the Packt Open Source brand, home to books published on software built around open source licenses, and offering information to anybody from advanced developers to budding web designers. The Open Source brand also runs Packt's Open Source Royalty Scheme, by which Packt gives a royalty to each open source project about whose software a book is sold.

Writing for Packt

We welcome all inquiries from people who are interested in authoring. Book proposals should be sent to author@packtpub.com. If your book idea is still at an early stage and you would like to discuss it first before writing a formal book proposal, then please contact us; one of our commissioning editors will get in touch with you.

We're not just looking for published authors; if you have strong technical skills but no writing experience, our experienced editors can help you develop a writing career, or simply get some additional reward for your expertise.

OpenCV Computer Vision with Python

ISBN: 978-1-78216-392-3 Paperback: 122 pages

Learn to capture videos, manipulate images, and track objects with Python using the OpenCV Library

1. Set up OpenCV, its Python bindings, and optional Kinect drivers on Windows, Mac or Ubuntu

2. Create an application that tracks and manipulates faces

3. Identify face regions using normal color images and depth images

OpenCV Computer Vision Application Programming Cookbook

Second Edition

ISBN: 978-1-78216-148-6 Paperback: 374 pages

Over 50 recipes to help you build computer vision applications in C++ using the OpenCV library

1. Master OpenCV, the open source library of the computer vision community.

2. Master fundamental concepts in computer vision and image processing.

3. Learn the important classes and functions of OpenCV with complete working examples applied on real images.

Please check **www.PacktPub.com** for information on our titles

OpenCV Computer Vision Application Programming [Video]

ISBN: 978-1-84969-488-9   Duration: 02:27 hours

Incorporate OpenCV's powerful computer vision application programming techniques to build and make your own applications stand out from the crowd

1. Learn everything you need to get started with OpenCV.

2. Contains many practical examples covering different areas of computer vision that can be mixed and matched to build your own application.

3. Packed with code with relevant explanation to demonstrate real results from real images.

OpenCV 3.0 Computer Vision with Java

ISBN: 978-1-78328-397-2   Paperback: 174 pages

Create multiplatform computer vision desktop and web applications using the combination of OpenCV and Java

1. Set up Java API for OpenCV to create popular Swing-based Graphical User Interfaces (GUIs).

2. Process videos and images in real-time with closer to native performance.

3. Make use of rock solid Java web application development practices to create engaging augmented reality experience and work with depth images from a Kinect device.

Please check **www.PacktPub.com** for information on our titles

Printed in Great Britain
by Amazon